Passport to Prayer

A Journey of Compassion

8-Week Bible Study and Prayer Experience for Women

Amber & Michael Van Schooneveld

"Never stop praying."
1 Thessalonians 5:17

Group
Incredible things will happen
Loveland, CO

Week 1

Prayer for the World

"'Because of the oppression of the weak and the groaning of the needy, I will now arise,' says the Lord." —Psalm 12:5

This first week, you'll begin to learn about the needs in this world and also what the Bible has to say about prayer for others. You'll ask God to soften and prepare your hearts for what he has in store for you in the next eight weeks.

Ask God to prepare your heart for this journey of compassion.

This study will guide you and your friends on an around-the-world adventure that takes you deeper into compassion and deeper into God's heart.

Stand in solidarity with your brothers and sisters in need around the world by experiencing what it might be like to eat on $1 a day, as millions of people do.

Week 2

Prayer for Uganda

"'He defended the cause of the poor and needy, and so all went well. Is that not what it means to know me?' declares the Lord." — Jeremiah 22:16

Uganda is a lush and fertile country in East Africa, long known as the "Pearl of Africa." But it also struggles with crippling issues, such as malaria and AIDS. This week you'll learn more about beautiful Uganda and how to pray for it.

Be reminded that the numbers and statistics we read about are really beautiful children like these!

"Whatever you did for one of the least of these brothers of mine, you did for me." Matthew 25:40

Fried Plantains With African Hot Sauce

- Vegetable oil
- 6 plantains
- Salt

Peel and thinly slice the plantains. (If the peel is hard, slice it off.) Heat enough oil to cover the bottom of a frying pan on medium heat. Add plantains. Fry several minutes on each side until lightly browned. Once cooked, place on paper towels, and salt to taste.
Serves 8 as an appetizer.

Experience an authentic African snack.

Week 3

Prayer for India

"There is neither Jew nor Greek, slave nor free, male nor female, for you are all one in Christ Jesus."
—Galatians 3:28

India is a vast country in South Asia brimming with beauty, different cultures, spiritual hunger, and needs. You'll engage in an Indian experience while learning more about the country and committing it to prayer.

Learn more about the plight of girls in India and how you can pray for them.

Indian Rice Pudding

- 2 cups cooked long grain white rice
- 2 cups whole milk
- 1 cup heavy cream
- 1 ½ cups coconut milk
- ½ cup sugar
- ½ teaspoon cardamom
- ⅔ cup golden raisins
- ⅔ cup chopped pistachios

Combine cooked rice and milk in a large saucepan on medium heat, and bring to a boil. Decrease heat to low and simmer about 5 minutes, stirring, until mixture begins to thicken.

Increase heat to medium and add heavy cream, coconut milk, sugar, and cardamom. Cook until mixture just begins to thicken, about 5 to 10 minutes. Remove from heat, and stir in raisins and pistachios. Serve at room temperature or chilled.

Week 4

Prayer for Haiti

"Suppose a brother or sister is without clothes and daily food. If one of you says to him, 'Go, I wish you well; keep warm and well fed,' but does nothing about his physical needs, what good is it? In the same way, faith by itself, if it is not accompanied by action, is dead." —James 2:15-17

This small country in the Caribbean was one of the first places where Columbus landed in the Americas, the second country in the Americas to declare independence, and the first country in the West to abolish slavery.

Learn how poor infrastructure and political instability are leaving children hungry.

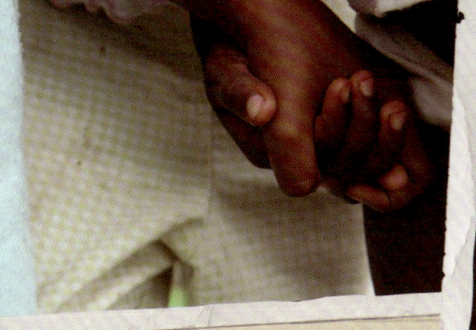
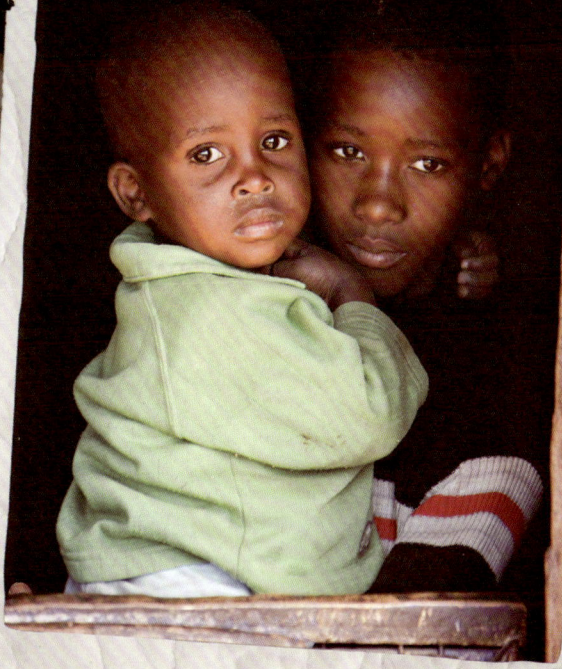

Haiti is a country with a proud past and a rich culture.

Soup Joumou (Pumpkin Soup)

- 4 cloves garlic
- 1 teaspoon thyme
- ¼ teaspoon black pepper
- 1 teaspoon salt
- 1 cup sliced green onions
- 1 pound of stew meat
- 3 quarts water
- 1 whole scotch bonnet or habanero pepper
- 1 pound pumpkin (or winter squash like butternut), peeled and chopped
- 2 carrots, peeled and sliced
- 2 stalks celery, chopped
- 1 large onion, chopped
- 2 medium turnips, cubed
- 4 potatoes, cubed
- 1 pound cabbage, finely chopped
- 4 ounces vermicelli pasta (or another thin pasta), broken in half
- 2 limes, juiced
- salt and pepper

See the full recipe on page 53.

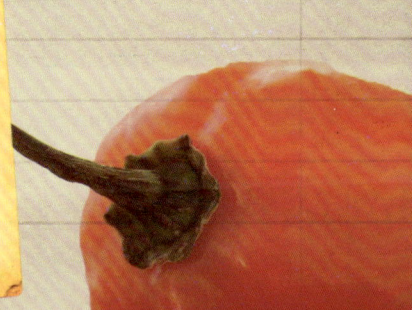

Week 5

Prayer for Thailand

"Whoever welcomes one of these little children in my name welcomes me." —Mark 9:37

Tropical Thailand is the only Southeast Asian country never to have been colonized. Although its economy is on the rise, it is still plagued by issues such as child trafficking and prostitution.

You'll pray for the little ones in danger of sex trafficking.

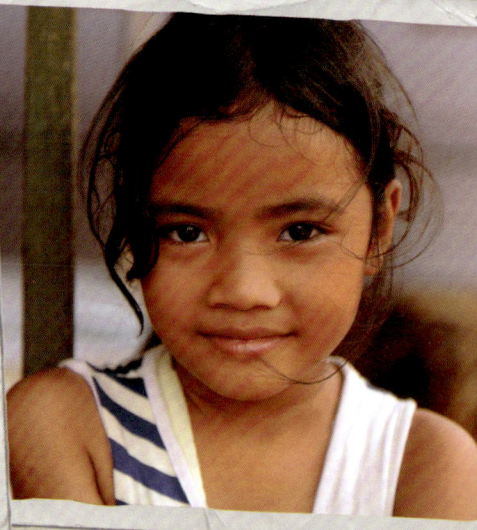

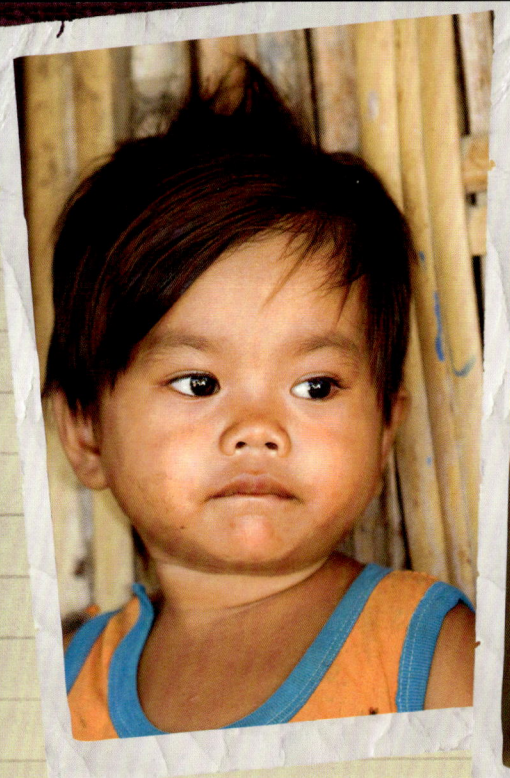

Mango Sticky Rice

See the full recipe on page 62.

Rice
- 1 ½ cups uncooked short-grain white rice
- 2 cups water
- 1 ½ cups light coconut milk
- ¾ cup sugar
- ½ teaspoon salt

Coconut Sauce
- ½ cup light coconut milk
- 1 tablespoon sugar
- ¼ teaspoon salt
- 1 tablespoon cornstarch

Toppings
- 3 mangoes, peeled and sliced
- 1 tablespoon toasted sesame seeds (optional)
- toasted coconut (optional)
- coconut ice cream (optional)

Week 6

Prayer for Bolivia

"Speak up for those who cannot speak for themselves, for the rights of all who are destitute. Speak up and judge fairly; defend the rights of the poor and needy." —Proverbs 31:8-9

Bolivia is a landlocked country in South America that is about one-and-a-half times the size of Texas. Though it has many natural resources and spans a diverse area ranging from steamy jungles to towering mountains and deserts, it is the poorest country in South America.

Pray for children in Bolivia who are at high risk of abuse and child labor.

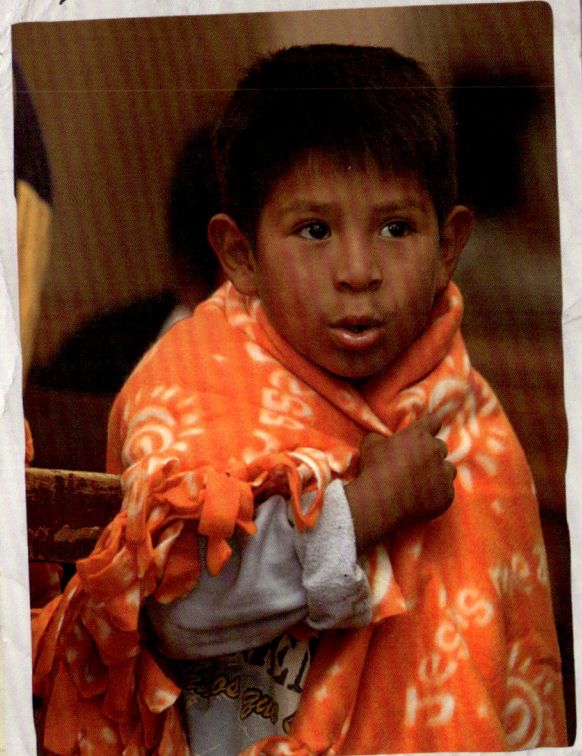

Cocadas

- 2 ⅔ cups sweetened shredded coconut
- ¾ cup sweetened condensed milk
- 1 egg
- ½ teaspoon almond extract

In a bowl, mix the coconut, egg, condensed milk, and almond extract. Let it stand for a couple of minutes. Cover the bottom of a baking sheet with parchment paper, and drop the mixture by teaspoons on the sheet. Bake at 325 degrees for 25 minutes or until golden and dry. Makes 24 candies.

Bolivian macaroon-like cookie

Week 7

Prayer for Afghanistan

"In fact, everyone who wants to live a godly life in Christ Jesus will be persecuted."
2 Timothy 3:12

Afghanistan is a rugged land of spectacular mountains that sits at the crossroads of Asia, Europe, and the Middle East. Decades of war and instability have left thousands unemployed and food insecurity high.

Pray for Christians in Afghanistan who live under threat of persecution and women who face enormous challenges.

Experience Afghan hospitality with dried apricots and pistachios and almonds.

Asabia el Aroos (Bride's Fingers)

- half of a 16-ounce package phyllo dough, thawed
- ¼ cup melted butter
- ½ cup almonds
- ⅓ cup sugar, plus extra to sprinkle on top
- 1 egg, beaten

To make filling, finely chop the almonds in a food processor and mix in ⅓ cup sugar. Cut the phyllo dough in half crosswise and in half again. Lay two of the rectangles stacked in front of you, with shorter sides toward you. (Cover remaining dough with a dampened towel.) Brush with butter. Put a tablespoon of filling in a line across the shorter side.

Fold in edges and then roll up like a cigar. Repeat with remaining dough and filling. Brush with the beaten egg, and sprinkle with sugar. Bake at 375 degrees for 15 to 20 minutes or until browned.

Week 8

Prayer for Vision

"For we are God's workmanship, created in Christ Jesus to do good works, which God prepared in advance for us to do"—Ephesians 2:10

This last week of your study, you'll reflect on how God has challenged you and changed you, and ask God to reveal to you what he has next for you—the works God has prepared in advance for you to do.

Group resources actually work!

This Group resource incorporates our R.E.A.L. approach to ministry. It reinforces a growing friendship with Jesus, encourages long-term learning, and results in life transformation, because it's

Relational
Learner-to-learner interaction enhances learning and builds Christian friendships.

Experiential
What learners experience through discussion and action sticks with them up to 9 times longer than what they simply hear or read.

Applicable
The aim of Christian education is to equip learners to be both hearers and doers of God's Word.

Learner-based
Learners understand and retain more when the learning process takes into consideration how they learn best.

Passport to Prayer
8-Week Bible Study and Prayer Experience for Women

Copyright © 2009 Amber and Michael Van Schooneveld
Visit our website: **group.com/women**

All rights reserved. No part of this book may be reproduced in any manner whatsoever without prior written permission from the publisher, except where noted in the text and in the case of brief quotations embodied in critical articles and reviews. For a permission request form, go to group.com/permissions, or write Women's Ministry Permissions, Group Publishing, Inc., P.O. Box 481, Loveland, CO 80539.

Credits
Authors: Amber and Michael Van Schooneveld
Executive Editor: Amy Nappa
Copy Editor: Janis Sampson and Ardeth Carlson
Chief Creative Officer: Joani Schultz
Art Director: Andrea Filer
Senior Designers: Kari Monson and Samantha Wranosky
Photography: Thom Schultz, Rodney Stewart, and iStockPhoto.com

Unless otherwise noted, Scripture taken from the Holy Bible, New International Version®, Copyright © 1973, 1978, 1984 by International Bible Society. Used by permission of Zondervan Publishing House. All rights reserved.

ISBN 978-0-7644-3840-0

10 9 8 7 6 5 4 3 2   18 17 16 15 14 13 12 11 10

Printed in Canada.

Contents

Your Passport 20

Using This Resource 21

Week 1: Prayer for the World 23

Week 2: Prayer for Uganda 32

Week 3: Prayer for India 42

Week 4: Prayer for Haiti 53

Week 5: Prayer for Thailand 62

Week 6: Prayer for Bolivia 74

Week 7: Prayer for Afghanistan 83

Week 8: Prayer for Vision 93

Day-to-Day Prayer Cards 99

Your Passport

Do you want to pray more for people around the world but aren't quite sure where to start? Well, this is your passport to prayer! This study will guide you and your friends on an around-the-world adventure that takes you deeper into compassion and deeper into God's heart.

We all want to pray more...but somehow it's always the thing that gets pushed to the end of our meetings, to the end of our days, and to the end of our to-do lists. This eight-week study will guide your small group, prayer group, or women's ministry to become intentional about prayer for the world—while building your friendships.

We also all want to know more about the issues in God's world that need our prayer—but we don't always know where to start, whom to listen to, or what to do about the issues once we know what they are. This guide will help you and your girlfriends learn more about the issues in the world that need our prayer, more about what the Bible has to say about them, and how to act in response to them.

Each small-group meeting will include tasty themed recipes and ideas for creating an international experience, a Bible study to learn more about what God's Word says, a prayer guide for your get-together, prayer cards for after your get-together, and ideas for action.

Each woman will need her own copy of this book. And if you're the hostess guiding the group, you'll find additional helps for you included here as well. It's easy!

So grab your girlfriends, your Bible, and get ready for a life-changing adventure!

Using This Resource

Who should do this eight-week study?

Small groups, prayer groups, or a women's ministry can use this resource together for a life-changing eight-week experience.

Who in your group needs to have this resource?

It's best for each woman to have her own copy of Passport to Prayer. This book has journaling sections and prayer cards for each woman to use throughout the week.

The Hostess pages will tell the hostess everything she needs to do to prepare for the get-together.

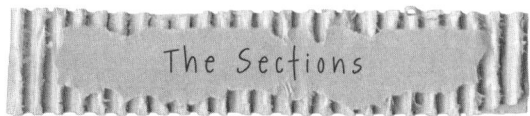
The Sections

Hostess Page

This page will give the hostess creative ideas for hosting the get-togethers, including...

A Taste of the Country

This section will give you a delicious recipe or two from the country you're praying for. Nothing brings people together like food—especially trying new international dishes together!

Creating the Country Experience

This section will give you ideas for creating a little corner of the world at your get-together, including decorating or cultural tips. These are easy ideas for adding ambience.

An Unforgettable Experience

This is an experience the hostess can do to make the get-together—and what God reveals to women—unforgettable. You won't want to miss these!

What the Bible Has to Say

This Bible study, which is done as a group, will bring direction to your prayers and help you know what the Bible says about the issues you're learning about. Allow God's Word to transform your minds and fuel your prayers. The study is meant to take just a short amount of time, around 10 minutes, so you can invest your time in prayer.

Prayer Time

Allow the Holy Spirit to guide your prayer time together…and use these prayer cues to nudge you in the right direction.

How you lead prayer is entirely up to you. Women can pray all together, in small groups, or even individually. You can formalize your prayer time—giving time cues as to what to pray when. For example, women can pray through each item one at a time as you call them out, or you can leave the entire time open for "popcorn" prayer, with women popping in their prayers as they feel led.

Try a mix to keep things fresh!

Ideas for Action

For each week there are a couple of ideas for action or resources to check out for more information. Reading about all the needs can be overwhelming; these ideas will help women know both how to pray and how to act in response to the needs. After your prayer time, if you or your friends are inspired to learn more or take some action, discuss these ideas together.

Day-to-Day Prayer Cards

These cards at the end of the book can be cut out to guide you and your friends to continue praying each day of the week after your get-together.

You can place the cards on a ring and carry them on your key chain, or post them in visible places around your home, work space, or car. You can pray through one each day of the week before your next meeting or activity.

Week 1: Prayer for the World

"'Because of the oppression of the weak and the groaning of the needy, I will now arise,' says the Lord." —Psalm 12:5

Hostess Page

Prayer for the World

This first week you'll study what the Bible has to say about prayer for others and ask God to prepare your hearts for this eight-week time of prayer.

A Taste of the World

At this first week you'll be asking God to prepare your hearts for the next eight weeks, so consider fasting for the day leading up to your first time together. Encourage each woman in your study to abstain from eating for the day and to pray during times of hunger. God can use this time of seeking him through fasting to soften your hearts as you prepare to have his heart for this world. This time of fasting will also make the Unforgettable Experience more powerful.

Unforgettable Experience

These Unforgettable Experiences will help your group understand and, in a small way, relate to the needs in the world. This first night together, you'll share a meal to help you connect with one another and to help you understand what it's like for many in need around the world.

Around the world, more than 1 billion people live on less than $1 a day, which is the measure of living in "absolute poverty." For your dinner together, create a meal that could be bought with the amount that a person living on $1 a day could afford.

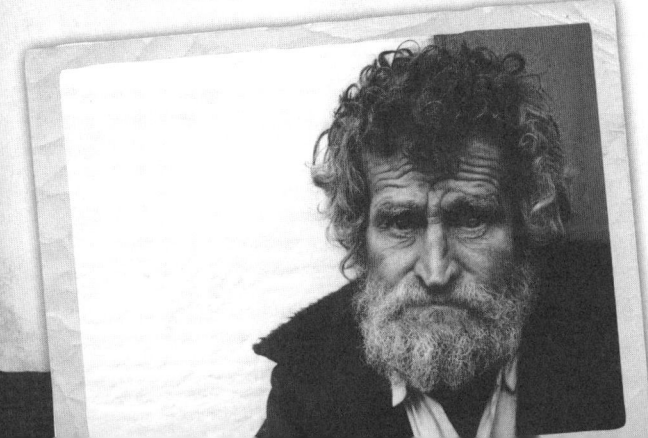

Week 1

Depending on the country, those living in poverty will spend 50% to 80% of their income on food and will likely eat only one to two meals a day. That gives you around 50 cents per person for the meal for this first week. A typical meal of those living in poverty that you could prepare would be a bowl of rice (about 3/4 cup per person) with a small side (about 1/2 cup) of vegetables (such as cooked greens) or fruit (such as mango). Serve water with the meal, but be sure to note to women that many of those living on $1 a day won't have access to clean water.

As you eat dinner together, discuss:

• How would you feel if this was your dinner, and perhaps only meal, every day?

• What would it take for you to feel satisfied after eating a meal like this?

• How does this meal change your perspective on what it's like to be poor?

WEEK 1

What the Bible Has to Say

This short Bible study will help you learn what the Bible has to say about prayer and those in need.

1. Pray

Open your time with a prayer that God would use this study, not to overwhelm you or make you feel guilt, but to soften your hearts toward those in need and to have his heart for this world.

2. Read and Discuss

Moving around your circle or room, have a different reader read each number and discuss the questions at the end of each reading. If you're in a larger group, form groups of four to six for this section.

Reader 1

There are many needs facing people around the world, and here are just some of them:

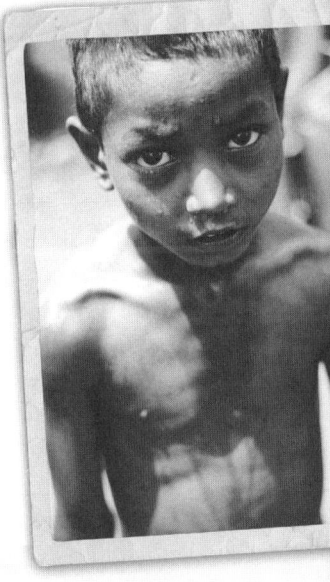

- There are 1.2 billion people in the world living in extreme poverty, on less than a dollar a day.

- There are 38.6 million people diagnosed with HIV worldwide.

- 1.2 million children are trafficked each year into exploitative labor.

- There are nearly 30,000 children under the age of 5 dying each day of hunger and preventable diseases.

Discuss

Clearly, there are many people in need around the world, but it's easy for the issues to seem distant or unreal. How easy or hard is it for you to connect with and care about the needs around the world? It's OK to be honest!

Reader 2

Psalm 12:5 says, "'Because of the oppression of the weak and the groaning of the needy, I will now arise,' says the Lord."

It's easy to get overwhelmed when we hear the statistics of need and oppression around the world, so it's important to find out what God's perspective is and what he would have us do about it.

Psalm 12:5 reminds us that God sees the plight of the weak and needy. The Bible also tells us that not only does God see their plight but he also cares for their plight.

Look up and read these Bible verses together:

- Proverbs 14:31
- Jeremiah 22:16
- James 1:27

Discuss

What do these verses help you understand about the character of God?

Reader 3

Psalm 12:5 also reminds us that God not only hears when people call out to him, he acts. It says, "Because of the…groaning of the needy, I will now arise." God acts, and he has also called us to act to help those in need.

Look up and read these Bible verses together:

- Exodus 3:7-8
- Isaiah 58:6-7

Discuss

- What actions do you see God doing in these passages?
- What do we learn from these verses about actions we can take to help those in need?

Reader 4

One of the greatest ways God exhorts us to act to care for those in need is through prayer. Prayer is a powerful weapon that God has given us in facing this world in need.

2 Corinthians 10:3-4 says, "We do not wage war as the world does. The weapons we fight with are not the weapons of the world. On the contrary, they have divine power to demolish strongholds."

Look up and read these Bible verses together:

- Ephesians 6:18
- 1 Thessalonians 5:17
- John 14:12-14

Discuss

- How do these verses affect your attitude toward these next weeks you'll spend in prayer for the needs in the world?
- How realistic do you think these verses are for you?

Write

What are your hopes for what God will do in these next eight weeks?

WEEK 1

Prayer Time

Tonight your prayer will focus on asking God to give you his heart for the world and those in need and to prepare you for these eight weeks of seeking him in prayer.

Tailor your prayer time to your group's size, location, and time. As these prayer cues are personal, you can allow time for people to pray through each cue individually; you can pray in a group with one or several people praying each cue; or you can have "popcorn" prayer with people praying as they feel led.

Prayer Cue 1

"But you, dear friends, build yourselves up in your most holy faith and pray in the Holy Spirit" (Jude 1:20).

Pray that God would fill you with his Holy Spirit as you pray for others and that these next eight weeks you would be praying in his will and through his strength and not your own.

Prayer Cue 2

"In this world you will have trouble. But take heart! I have overcome the world" (John 16:33).

Pray that you wouldn't become overwhelmed as you learn about the needs in the world but that God would help you take heart, knowing that Christ has overcome this world. Pray that God would give you his peace and his love for this world.

Prayer Cue 3

"Looking at his disciples, he said: 'Blessed are you who are poor, for yours is the kingdom of God. Blessed are you who hunger now, for you will be satisfied. Blessed are you who weep now, for you will laugh'" (Luke 6:20-21).

Pray that God would help you view the poor, those who are weak and in need, the way he views them. Pray that God would help you have the attitude that he has for those in need.

Prayer Cue 4

"The apostles said to the Lord, 'Increase our faith!' He replied, 'If you have faith as small as a mustard seed, you can say to this mulberry tree, "Be uprooted and planted in the sea," and it will obey you'" (Luke 17:5-6).

Pray that God would increase your faith, that you would believe in his power to "demolish strongholds" in this world of need through your prayers.

Prayer Cue 5

"And pray in the Spirit on all occasions with all kinds of prayers and requests. With this in mind, be alert and always keep on praying for all the saints" (Ephesians 6:18).

Pray that God would give you strength and lasting passion through the Holy Spirit to pray continually for others. Pray that God would help you be alert and always keep on praying.

Prayer Cue 6

"And whatever you do, whether in word or deed, do it all in the name of the Lord Jesus, giving thanks to God the Father through him" (Colossians 3:17).

Commit the next eight weeks to God, asking that he would use this time to change you and the world around you.

WEEK 1

Closing

Remind each person to use the Prayer Cards at the end of this book to pray during this next week.

Ideas for Action

- Cut out the Prayer Cards at the end of the book for Week 1, and use these cards to continue praying each day this week.

- Consider reading *Hope Lives: A Journey of Restoration* to understand more about God's heart for the poor and how he calls us to respond as Christians.

Week 2: Prayer for Uganda

"'He defended the cause of the poor and needy, and so all went well. Is that not what it means to know me?' declares the Lord." — Jeremiah 22:16

Hostess Page

Prayer for Uganda

Uganda is a lush and fertile country in East Africa, long known as the Pearl of Africa. But it also struggles with a number of crippling issues, such as malaria and AIDS. This week you'll learn more about beautiful Uganda and how to pray for it.

A Taste of Uganda

Uganda is one of the top producers in the world of plantains, a staple of the African diet. Plantains are like bananas but more starchy and less sweet. You'll find them in the produce section of your grocery store, next to the bananas. You can use them when they're green (less ripe) or when they start to brown (more ripe). The riper they are the sweeter they will be.

You can serve them alone or with an African hot sauce.

Fried Plantains With African Hot Sauce

- ○ Vegetable oil
- ○ 6 plantains
- ○ Salt

Peel and thinly slice the plantains. (If the peel is hard, slice it off.) Heat enough oil to cover the bottom of a frying pan on medium heat. Add plantains. Fry several minutes on each side until lightly browned. Once cooked, place on paper towels, and salt to taste. Serves 8 as an appetizer.

Week 2

African Hot Sauce

- one 8-ounce can tomato sauce
- ¼ cup chopped onion
- 1 clove garlic
- 3 tablespoons lemon juice
- 4 to 8 fresh red jalapeño chilies (Use chilies according to how hot you want your sauce.)

Remove all the seeds from the chilies, and using a knife, cut out the veins. (This is where a lot of heat is!) Chop the onion and chilies. Puree all ingredients in a blender or food processor, adding one chili at a time to test for heat.

Creating the Ugandan Experience

- So your guests can learn more about Uganda and get to know more about one another, cut out and copy the Uganda Cards at the end of this book. Place them around your meeting area for women to read and answer while eating snacks. Or you can read them aloud to your guests for everyone to answer together as an icebreaker.

- Coffee makes up the majority of Uganda's exports. While eating your plantains, consider serving some Ugandan coffee. You can buy Ugandan coffee from nonprofit organizations that work to develop and maintain income-generating activities in poverty-stricken areas. Visit ugandangold.com to learn more and buy some for your group. (And you can even see the picture of the farmers who will be harvesting your coffee!)

Week 2

Unforgettable Experience

At this meeting, you'll learn more about the devastating impact malaria is having on Uganda and Africa. Often numbers don't really sink in with us—we can't really experience a couple of digits on a page. Here's an idea that will illustrate how real these numbers are.

After you've enjoyed the snacks, begin your time together by introducing the topic of malaria.

Here's what you'll need:

- 3,000 metal BBs (You can buy BBs in bulk online or at sporting goods stores for under or around $10.)
- pitcher
- large metal pot or basin

Say: Today we're going to pray for Uganda, a lush and fertile country, which has long been called the Pearl of Africa.

One serious issue facing Uganda is malaria. Malaria is the leading cause of death in Uganda, and one in six children in Uganda die of malaria.

In the world, over 1 million people die each year from this treatable and preventable disease, mainly children under 5 in sub-Saharan Africa.

It's hard to understand how many people over 1 million a year is. It is equal to almost 3,000 a day. To illustrate how many this is, I'm going to pour one BB per person into this metal basin. Listen carefully to the sound, and ask God to touch your heart with this experience. As each BB hits the metal, realize that each "ping" represents a person or child who died too soon and unnecessarily.

Week 2

Slowly pour each of the BBs from your pitcher into the basin. (You might want to practice this before your meeting so you know how fast you want to pour.)

After all are poured, discuss: What impact does this illustration have on you? How does this help you put perspective on the problem in Uganda?

Give each person one BB to keep. Each woman can put the BB in her pocket or on her desk as a reminder that those in need around the world are real people and as a reminder to pray.

A Note From Amber

I work at an organization whose mission is to release children from poverty, so I hear the numbers of poverty every day. But when I experienced this activity at a meeting, it brought me to tears. God used it to bring my heart alive to the lives of those who would otherwise be statistics.

WEEK 2

What the Bible Has to Say

This short Bible study will help you hear God's Word for helping those in need. Moving around your circle or room, have a different person read each numbered segment, and as a group discuss the questions at the end of each reading. If you're in a larger group, form groups of four to six for this section.

Reader 1

Many worship songs that Christians sing have a lyric similar to this: "Lord, I want to know you more." Many Christian books have been written about how we can serve God with all our hearts. Many of us want to know God and serve him with all our hearts.

> *Discuss*
>
> What do you do to get to know God more?

Reader 2

The Bible gives us clues for how we can know God more and serve him.

Jeremiah 22:16 says, "'He defended the cause of the poor and needy, and so all went well. Is that not what it means to know me?' declares the Lord."

> *Discuss*
>
> How do you think defending the cause of the poor and needy helps you to know God?

Reader 3

Matthew 25:34-40 says, "Then the King will say to those on his right, 'Come, you who are blessed by my Father; take your inheritance, the kingdom prepared for you since the creation of the world. For I was hungry and you gave me something to eat, I was thirsty and you gave me something to drink, I was a stranger and you invited me in, I needed clothes and you clothed me, I was sick and you looked after me, I was in prison and you came to visit me.'

"Then the righteous will answer him, 'Lord, when did we see you hungry and feed you, or thirsty and give you something to drink? When did we see you a stranger and invite you in, or needing clothes and clothe you? When did we see you sick or in prison and go to visit you?' The King will reply, 'I tell you the truth, whatever you did for one of the least of these brothers of mine, you did for me.'"

Discuss

- What do you think this means or how would you explain this to someone else?

- Why do you think so many passages in the Bible equate serving the poor with serving God?

Reader 4

Proverbs 19:17 says, "He who is kind to the poor lends to the Lord."

Discuss

How does reading this verse and the others before it impact the way you view people in other countries in need? For example, how might it change the way you view children in Uganda who are dying from malaria?

Write your prayer to God for the way you'd like him to use these verses to change your perspective on those in need around the world.

WEEK 2

Prayer Time

This week you'll read through each prayer cue and then spend time praying for the needs reflected in each one. Have one person read each cue, and then pray together for the needs before moving on to the next cue.

Prayer Cue 1

Malaria is a preventable, treatable disease that is the leading cause of death in Uganda, though not everyone dies who gets malaria. Those who get malaria and survive are generally sick for 10 to 20 days.

Most adults who get malaria are day laborers, who each earn less than $1 or $2 a day and use the money they earn each day to buy their families food. But when they get malaria, they can't work or provide for their families.

Children who get malaria miss school for long periods of time, and some aren't able to properly develop socially because of permanent neurological damage from the disease. Parents whose children get malaria can't work to provide them with food because the parents stay home to care for their children. In Uganda just the reported cases of malaria amount to 65 million a year in a country with a population of just around 28 million! That means each person is getting malaria multiple times a year. When such a significant amount of the population is ill and unable to work, it traps them in a cycle of poverty.

Malaria is transmitted through mosquitoes that bite at night, so insecticide-treated bed nets can drastically lower the cases of malaria. Even though a bed net costs only $5 to $10, it's still out of reach for the majority of the people in Uganda, who make less than $1 a day and might not have had any education on preventing malaria.

Spend some time praying together for effective malaria prevention, that the government and other organizations would be able to effectively educate on malaria prevention and get funds to distribute bed nets. Pray for those who are suffering from malaria.

Encouraging Thought

It's easy to be overwhelmed by the huge numbers of those suffering from malaria, but there's definitely hope, as malaria is such a preventable disease. The President's Malaria Initiative, which began in 2005, distributes nets and provides malaria prevention education in Africa. It has already in some areas of implementation brought the levels of malaria infection in children down 90% since being implemented.

Prayer Cue 2: Political Stability and Recovery

There have been numerous armed conflicts in Uganda in the past several decades, and the country is still recovering from the negative impact of the military dictatorship of Idi Amin in the 1970s, which resulted in the killing of an estimated 300,000 people.

There are 1.27 million internally displaced persons in Uganda who live in camps, people who have been forced to leave their homes because of fighting. Those living in these camps are in conditions of extreme poverty, are vulnerable to attack, and often lack means to generate an income.

Pray for those who have been impacted by war. Pray for a final and lasting peace. Pray for a government that shuns corruption and puts the good of its people first.

Pray that those displaced would be able to safely return home and become self-supporting. Pray that the children displaced by war would have access to health care and education through the help of the government and aid organizations.

Prayer Cue 3: AIDS

AIDS is one of the leading causes of death of adults in Uganda. Since the first case of AIDS in Uganda was detected in 1982, 2.6 million Ugandans have been diagnosed with AIDS, and 1.6 million have died. This has left nearly 1 million orphans in Uganda.

Effective preventive measures through the government and nonprofit organizations did create a decrease in infections from 18% in 1992 to 6% in 2002, although infection rates may now be rising again.

Those who have AIDS and their families often suffer stigma in their communities, becoming outcasts and suffering discrimination.

Pray for effective education and prevention of AIDS. Pray that the government and nonprofit organizations make wise decisions about how to address the issue. Pray for those who have AIDS and are suffering discrimination. Pray for the orphans AIDS has left behind.

Prayer Cue 4: Vulnerable Children

AIDS has left a large number of orphans in Uganda and street children in Kampala. During the wars of the past several decades, approximately 25,000 children have also been kidnapped to serve as child soldiers or as sex slaves.

During this time, night commuting became common in Northern Uganda, children fleeing at night to cities to escape physical harm or kidnapping. Night commuting is decreasing, although it is still occurring in some areas.

Pray for the spiritual, emotional, physical, and social welfare of these children. Pray that God would place responsible and caring adults in their lives and that they would be integrated back into society.

Prayer Cue 5: Prayer for the Church

Uganda's population is 42% Protestant, and another 42% is Catholic; 12% is Muslim. Although there was religious persecution under Idi Amin, there is now religious freedom.

Pray for the unity of the Ugandan church, between denominations and tribes. Pray that the churches would rely on God's strength and Holy Spirit.

Pray that the church would be able to respond to the needs of its country with God's grace. Pray that Ugandan Christians would be able to share the good news of God's grace with their Muslim neighbors.

Prayer Cue 6: Food Insecurity

Uganda is a fertile agricultural country, and many of the surrounding countries depend on it for food. But with rising fuel and food prices, it becomes difficult for those living in poverty to afford even their daily meals. In some places agricultural practices that aren't environmentally sustainable are used. Natural disasters, such as heavy rains or drought, can also destroy crops each year.

Pray that sustainable agricultural practices would be used by farmers. Pray for the success of small-scale agricultural ventures for subsistence farmers. Pray for a long-term solution to the global rising cost of fuel and food.

Closing

To end your time together, remind each person of the BB she put in her pocket to remember those who are in need in Uganda. Remind each woman to use the Prayer Cards at the end of this book to keep praying throughout the week.

Ideas for Action

- Cut out the Prayer Cards at the end of the book for Week 2, and use these cards to continue praying each day this week for Uganda.

- Read more about Invisible Children, an organization that seeks to help children in Northern Uganda who have been affected by war, and consider watching the movie about night commuting. Visit invisiblechildren.com.

- Donate an insecticide-treated bed net to keep one child healthy and alive in Uganda. A donation of $10 to **Malaria No More** will buy a net and pay for distribution and education on how to use it. Visit malarianomore.org.

Week 3: Prayer for India

"There is neither Jew nor Greek, slave nor free, male nor female, for you are all one in Christ Jesus."
—Galatians 3:28

Hostess Page

Prayer for India

India is a vast country in South Asia brimming with beauty, different cultures, spiritual hunger, and needs. You'll engage in an Indian experience while learning more about the country and committing it to prayer.

A Taste of India

Here's a recipe for authentic chai, a traditional drink of India…but if you want to go a bit easy on yourself, buy a box of chai concentrate at the grocery store and follow the instructions on the box. Serve it with Indian Rice Pudding. Rice pudding is a popular dessert throughout Asia. If you want to make things even simpler, use store-bought rice pudding and mix in ⅔ cup raisins, ⅔ cup chopped pistachios, and ¼ teaspoon ground cardamom per 8 servings.

Masala Chai

- 4 cups water
- 4 cups milk
- ½ teaspoon cardamom seeds
- ½ teaspoon whole black peppercorns
- ½ teaspoon whole cloves
- 1 cinnamon stick
- 2-inch stick fresh ginger
- 4 teaspoons loose black tea leaves
- 8 ounces honey

Bring water and milk to a boil in a saucepan. Add all remaining ingredients except honey, and turn the heat to low. Simmer covered for 10 minutes. Remove from heat and strain. Add honey and mix well. Can be served hot or cold.

Week 3

Indian Rice Pudding

- 2 cups cooked long grain white rice
- 2 cups whole milk
- 1 cup heavy cream
- 1½ cups coconut milk
- ½ cup sugar
- ½ teaspoon cardamom
- ⅔ cup golden raisins
- ⅔ cup chopped pistachios

Combine cooked rice and milk in a large saucepan on medium heat, and bring to a boil. Decrease heat to low and simmer about 5 minutes, stirring, until mixture begins to thicken.

Increase heat to medium and add heavy cream, coconut milk, sugar, and cardamom. Cook until mixture just begins to thicken, about 5 to 10 minutes. Remove from heat, and stir in raisins and pistachios. Serve at room temperature or chilled.

Creating the Indian Experience

- During your get-together, consider having your friends sit on the floor. In India, this posture is assumed as an acknowledgment of the divine and as a symbol of surrender. Explain this to your friends, and ask that you all have a mindfulness of the presence of God and an attitude of surrender to him during your get-together.

- In many rural Indian churches, people leave their shoes at the door and sit cross-legged on the floor on mattresses or sheets. Prepare a sign at the door showing people where to leave their shoes. Place colorful sheets in the middle of your room for your prayer area. (And this will help you relate to those churches who don't own chairs for their members to sit on!)

- To add some additional Indian ambience to your get-together, you can burn incense, or burn spice-, wood-, or mango-scented candles. (Mangoes are the national fruit. For an easy side dish to your treats, serve mango chunks.)

Week 3

Unforgettable Experience

At this get-together, you'll learn more about the discrimination that many girls in India face. To help relate to this issue and to get to know each other better, begin your meeting with this icebreaker.

Give each person a sheet of newsprint and some markers, and tell the women you're going to create childhood timelines. Each person will draw a timeline of the events in her life from when she was born until she was 18. Ask everyone to include things such as what her favorite birthday was, what her dream in high school was, or what her favorite thing to do as a teenager or child was. It's OK if the "events" they include aren't very newsworthy. Things like "played soccer a lot" or "competed in gymnastics" or "loved the Transformers" are all fine.

Once everyone has drawn a timeline, have each woman share what she drew. (If you're in a large group, form smaller groups of four or five for this activity.)

After each person has had a chance to share, read this.

Say: Childhood should be a time of learning and growing in a safe environment. Today we're going to learn more about India and the issues facing it. One of the issues facing India is the treatment of girls who don't grow up in a carefree environment.

In some parts of India, many girls are married off and begin having children when they are just teenagers, even as young as 13 years old. Many girls aren't fed enough because they're less important than the boys in the family. Many have no chance to experience childhood or receive an education, but instead they get stuck in a cycle of poverty. Today we're going to pray for these little girls whom God wants to be able to just be children.

WEEK 3

Learning About India

Read through these pages together to learn more about India and its needs, having a different woman read each section. You can read it together as a group or in smaller groups.

Reader 1

About India

There are almost 1.15 billion people in India—80.5% are Hindu, 13.4% are Muslim, and 2.3% are Christian. India is the seventh largest country in the world and the second most populous country. It's one of the fastest-growing economies in the world, but it is still marked by high levels of poverty, illiteracy, malnutrition, and environmental degradation.

Civilization in India dates back to at least 3300 B.C., with many dynasties coming and going. Lured by the trade routes, Europeans were drawn to India by the 16th century and eventually established colonies. By 1857 the British Crown claimed India as a colony of the British Empire. India didn't gain its independence until 1947, after decades of nonviolent protests led by Mahatma Gandhi.

The government of India is now a democratic republic—the largest democracy in the world.

Reader 2

Some of the Needs of India

Though recent laws have attempted to outlaw discrimination, the Hindu caste system still leaves certain groups of people intimidated, poor, and persecuted. Caste affects who you can marry, what profession you can pursue, and even where you can get your water.

Reader 3

Seventy percent of all Christian Indians are of the Dalit castes, and the average Hindu, therefore, associates the gospel with the untouchables. Hindu extremism in the past has also called for an "only Hindu" India, using violence against Muslims and Christians. An incidence of persecution against Christians occurs every 36 hours in India.

Reader 4

India has more and larger people groups with no Christians, churches, or Christian workers than any other part of the world. The majority of Christians are situated in the south, and only 5% of Christian Indians live in the more populous north and west where these huge unreached people groups live.

Reader 5

About 286 million people in India earn less than 40 cents a day, the government's poverty threshold.

Reader 6

Spotlight Need: The Eradication of Discrimination Against Girls

There is a deficit of 35 million women in India, partly because of female infanticide and abortion. Although the Indian government has been working to end discrimination against girls, the plight of girls in India is still bleak, especially because of ingrained and accepted cultural practices.

Reader 7

In poor Indian families, boys are much easier on a family than girls. Having a boy proves a father's manhood and brings him honor. And beyond that, according to some Indian customs, one must have a son to perform the parents' funeral rites or the entry into the next life will not be blessed.

A father may not feel as blessed with a daughter because he'll have to pay exorbitant amounts for her dowry—far more than any poor family can afford (even though dowries are outlawed by the government). So another girl is another dowry to be paid that you can't afford and another mouth to feed—a sometimes unwelcome mouth when all you really wanted was a boy. Some women will encourage one another to kill their coming female infant and hope for a boy next time.

Reader 8

If the girl makes it past the womb and there happens to be brothers around, she'll likely be fed less or sometimes starved if there isn't enough to go around. Discrimination against girls in feeding contributes to the 45% of children younger than 3 who are undernourished in India. If there is money for school fees, it will more likely go to the brothers, while the girls will likely remain illiterate and uneducated.

Living in poor, rural areas, it isn't uncommon for a girl to be given as a child bride. Many girls will be trafficked into the cities for labor, to be given as child brides, or for commercial sexual exploitation. It is unlikely that a woman will ever own any land.

Reader 9

What hope can there be for these girls whose futures look so bleak? Only the hope of Christ—Christ's power to transform cultures and people and to crush strongholds. And the power of prayer.

In Romans 15:30, Paul says, "I urge you, brothers, by our Lord Jesus Christ and by the love of the Spirit, to join me in my struggle by praying to God for me."

We aren't helpless to help these girls. In prayer we're joining with them in their struggle. We're standing up next to them and pleading for them, and we know that God will hear us.

WEEK 3

What the Bible Has to Say

If your group is large, form groups of four to five for this short Bible study that will help you hear God's Word and God's hope for girls in India and guide your prayer. Have a different person read each numbered section. Take about 10 minutes for this so you'll have plenty of time to pray.

Reader 1

Galatians 3:26-29 says, "You are all sons of God through faith in Christ Jesus, for all of you who were baptized into Christ have clothed yourselves with Christ. There is neither Jew nor Greek, slave nor free, male nor female, for you are all one in Christ Jesus. If you belong to Christ, then you are Abraham's seed, and heirs according to the promise."

No matter if it's a girl destitute in India, a modern-day slave, or a foreigner in a land far away from here, each is so significant that Christ died for them and invites them to be his heirs.

There are no throw-away people—God wants each little girl to be his princess. Sometimes it's easy to view the countless numbers of those oppressed and poor in faraway places as just faceless statistics in inevitable poverty.

> *Discuss*
>
> When you hear about the numbers of those in need in other places, do you think of them the same way you would think of someone in this country—your mother or sister or friend or neighbor?

Reader 2

Jeremiah 29:11 says, "'For I know the plans I have for you,' declares the Lord, 'plans to prosper you and not to harm you, plans to give you hope and a future.'"

We may hear this verse often, that God has a good plan for our lives. Although this can be hard to believe, it's easier to consider in the context of the many opportunities in this country. But instead of applying this verse to yourself, apply it to these girls in India.

Write

Do you believe that God has a good plan he wants for each of their lives? Do you believe that God has ideas and dreams and hopes for each child, who could easily be considered an inevitable drop in the bucket of poverty?

Go back to your timeline that you created earlier. Look at your own life. Based on what you know of the girls in India, put an X through every item that a girl in India is unlikely to have experienced.

Reflect on the life of these girls. How are they like you?
How are they different from you?

Discuss

- Does it come naturally to you to apply Jeremiah 29:11 to the girls in India?
- How can we allow God to transform our minds to view these girls as he views them?

WEEK 3

Prayer Time

After the Bible study, you can pray in one big group or smaller groups or individually. You can also split your prayer time into short chunks, tackling one prayer cue at a time, or you can have one long, uninterrupted time.

Each group can tackle one prayer cue to concentrate more deeply, or each group can work through each cue.

Prayer Cue 1

Praise God for the Indian church—its leaders, preachers, writers, and apologists. Thank God for the church across India that is growing in unity and maturity through persecution.

Prayer Cue 2

Many in India don't know a single Christian and have no idea what Jesus' good news is. Pray for workers and for the harvest.

"[Jesus] told them, 'The harvest is plentiful, but the workers are few. Ask the Lord of the harvest, therefore, to send out workers into his harvest field'" (Luke 10:2).

Pray for the North India Ganges Plain, where there are few Christians to share the gospel. Pray for the people groups and castes that have virtually no link to the gospel.

Prayer Cue 3

Hindu militants and mobs are responsible for beatings (sometimes resulting in death) of pastors and pastors' wives. Homes and churches are burnt, prayer meetings are attacked, and those who speak of Christ are threatened.

Pray that freedom of religion would be recognized throughout India.

Pray for the protection of pastors, evangelists, and Christians as they share the good news of Christ. Pray for the protection of those who turn to Christ.

Pray that those persecuting Christians would experience the grace and love of Jesus Christ through the Christians they persecute.

Prayer Cue 4

Child abuse is rampant in India, and there are 70 million child laborers and 10 million bonded laborers—children in a form of slavery to pay off family debt. There are over a half million child prostitutes.

Pray for child advocacy efforts to succeed—that children would be educated about their rights and that justice would be upheld in the judicial system.

Pray for healing for those abused, that God would place in their lives a trusted adult in whom they can confide, that they would find comfort in God.

Prayer Cue 5

Astounding numbers of Indians live on the streets, eat one meal a day or less, and have little access to sanitation, health care, education, or opportunity.

Pray that the cycle of poverty would be broken in the lives of India's children. Pray that the efforts of the government and aid organizations would be effective, full of integrity, and implemented well.

Pray that God would show those in poverty that he loves them, values them, and has a good plan for their lives.

Pray that those in backward castes or the Dalit caste would have equal rights recognized and gain opportunities.

Prayer Cue 6

Pray that the Holy Spirit would transform through the power of Christ and his church a society that devalues, exploits, and oppresses girls.

Pray that the government would continue to ensure the rights of girls and would enforce these rights.

Pray that girls would believe in their value and would be educated of their rights so that they will beware of those seeking to traffic or exploit them.

Pray that they would be enabled to remain in school. Pray that the dowry practice would become less and less prevalent.

Pray that men would stand up and speak out for the rights of girls and women.

Closing

Remind each woman to cut out the Prayer Cards at the end of the book to keep praying for India throughout the week.

Ideas for Action

- Cut out the Prayer Cards at the end of the book for Week 3, and use these cards to continue praying each day this week for India.

- Opportunity International is a Christian organization that provides opportunities to those in chronic poverty, especially women. You can donate any amount of money to be given as small-business loans to women in India. Opportunity International will provide training and counseling to empower them to create self-generating income. Even $15 can help a woman in India start a new and hopeful chapter in her life. See opportunity.org.

- Show girls in your own area how valuable they are by volunteering to tutor at programs for disadvantaged students or students with learning disabilities.

- Remind a girl in your own life of her incredible value as a daughter of God by making her a card—celebrating her incredible worth and beauty and promise in Christ.

Week 4: Prayer for Haiti

"Suppose a brother or sister is without clothes and daily food. If one of you says to him, 'go, I wish you well; keep warm and well fed,' but does nothing about his physical needs, what good is it? In the same way, faith by itself, if it is not accompanied by action, is dead." —James 2:15-17

Hostess Page

Prayer for Haiti

This small country in the Caribbean was one of the first places where Columbus landed in the Americas, the second country in the Americas to declare independence, and the first country in the West to abolish slavery.

A Taste of Haiti

Pumpkin soup is the traditional dish eaten on Haiti's Independence Day. Read the Unforgettable Experience section to learn more about it. (Thank you to my Haitian friend Ephraim Lindor for the recipe!) Serve this to women to give them a bit of flavor from the country. This recipe makes a lot of soup. You may want to halve the recipe.

Soup Joumou (Pumpkin Soup)

- 4 cloves garlic, minced
- 1 teaspoon thyme
- ¼ teaspoon black pepper
- 1 teaspoon salt
- 1 cup sliced green onions
- 1 pound of stew meat
- 3 quarts water
- 1 whole scotch bonnet or habanero pepper
- 1 pound pumpkin (or winter squash like butternut), peeled and chopped
- 2 carrots, peeled and sliced
- 2 stalks celery, chopped
- 1 large onion, chopped
- 2 medium turnips, cubed
- 4 potatoes, cubed
- 1 pound cabbage, finely chopped
- 4 ounces vermicelli pasta (or another thin pasta), broken in half
- 2 limes, juiced
- salt and pepper

Week 4

Soup Joumou (Pumpkin Soup) cont.

Combine the first five ingredients in a large plastic bag. Add the stew meat and shake to coat the meat. Leave in the bag for an hour. Bring the water to a boil in a large pot, and add the meat and chili pepper. Cover, reduce heat, and simmer for 2 hours. Remove the meat and set aside. Remove the pepper and discard.

Add the pumpkin and carrots, and cook covered until very tender, about 20 minutes. Puree the pumpkin and carrots in the broth, using an immersion blender. Or puree in a standard blender and pour back into the pot. (You may need to do this in several batches.) Add the meat back to the pot.

Add the celery, onion, turnips, and potato to the soup, bring to a boil, and then reduce heat and simmer for 15 minutes. Thin the broth with as much water as needed—it should not be too thick.

Add cabbage and cook 15 more minutes. Add the vermicelli and cook until it is tender. Thin again with water as needed. Stir in the lime juice. Season with salt and pepper.

Creating the Haitian Experience

- Haiti is known for its great music. If you'd like to add a little cultural flair to your get-togethers, visit putumayo.com, which offers music CDs from all around the world, including Haitian and Caribbean music. (And part of the proceeds will go to nonprofits around the world.) Listen to the tunes of Haiti while eating the famous Haitian dish Soup Joumou.

Unforgettable Experience

Eating your Soup Joumou can be a great way to learn a little more about the history of Haiti. As you eat, tell your guests about the history of the soup:

Haiti, the western part of the island of Hispaniola in the Caribbean (the Dominican Republic is on the eastern half), was claimed by the French in the 1600s. Hundreds of thousands of slaves (some say almost a million) were brought from Africa to Haiti to work crops such as coffee and sugar. It was so productive, one of the richest colonies in the French Empire, that it was called the Pearl of the Antilles.

Week 4

But the slaves, who had been living in deplorable conditions, revolted, and after much fighting, on January 1, 1804, they claimed independence from France and abolished slavery—the second country in the Americas to gain independence from their colonizers and the first country to abolish slavery.

To celebrate, the former slaves ate pumpkin soup, which was a dish only the colonizers ate. They ate it to show that they were equal to all. It is still a tradition to eat pumpkin soup on January 1 as a symbol of freedom and brotherhood.

The achievement of the slaves in gaining independence in Haiti was influential in American history, as it encouraged the abolition of slavery in the U.S. Haiti also played an important role in defeating the French attempt at expansion in the Americas, leaving the West open for expansion by the United States.

Although Haiti was a model for America in abolishing slavery, its history for the past 200 years has been marked by bloodshed, corruption, and poverty.

Haiti is the poorest, least developed nation in the Western Hemisphere. Its government is perceived as one of the most corrupt in the world, and it has been made unstable by multiple coups and changes in government.

Have your guests turn to the next page and read the quote by Fredrick Douglass. Then as a group, discuss the questions following it.

WEEK 4

Learning About and Praying for Haiti

Read this quote by Fredrick Douglass, a former American slave who became a statesman and the U.S. ambassador to Haiti:

> "Until she spoke, no Christian nation had abolished Negro slavery...Until she spoke, the slave ship, followed by hungry sharks, greedy to devour the dead and dying slaves flung overboard to feed them, ploughed in peace the South Atlantic, painting the sea with the Negro's blood. Until she spoke, the slave trade was sanctioned by all the Christian nations of the world, and our land of liberty and light included. Men made fortunes by this infernal traffic, and were esteemed as good Christians...Until Haiti spoke, the church was silent, and the pulpit was dumb. In forecasting the future of this people, then, I insist that some importance shall be given to this and to another grand initial fact: that the freedom of Haiti was not given as a boon, but conquered as a right! Her people fought for it. They suffered for it...and perished for it."

Discuss

- How does learning more about Haiti's history and knowing about America's shared history with Haiti change your perspective of it?
- How does it change your perception of the people?

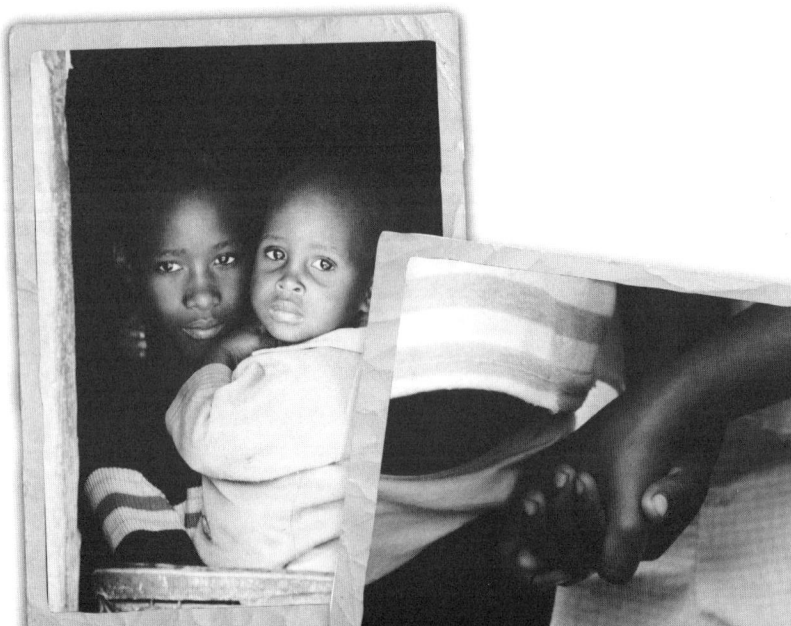

Read and Pray

Read this together, or in small groups, having a different reader read each section. This week you'll pray together as you learn more about each issue.

Reader 1

Two serious problems facing Haiti are the instability of the government and government corruption. Haiti has a history of government leaders not completing their terms because of coups, rebellions, and violence. American forces occupied it from 1915 to 1934, and since then it has suffered from a succession of dictators and revolts.

As a result, crime is high, the infrastructure is deteriorating, the police force is ineffective, corruption is pervasive, and the government is unable to address the needs of the people, such as basic education and health care.

Pray

Take time to pray for the government of Haiti. Pray for incorruptible, wise leaders to come to power who genuinely want to serve their people and bring change to their country.

Pray for stability, that the leaders can find long-term solutions to the poverty and other issues that plague the country.

Reader 2

Haiti was once the richest French colony in the new world. Now, because of deforestation, Haiti has less than 2% of its tree cover, resulting in terrible soil erosion that renders the land unusable. This leads to further flooding, landslides, and deaths when heavy rains occur.

The destruction of forests, government instability, and lack of infrastructure have also contributed to the decline of tourism and investment in the country, both important staples of the economy in the Caribbean.

Pray

Pray for the healing of the land. Pray for education in sustainable farming and agricultural practices. Pray for effective government enforcement of environmental policies and solutions to the huge environmental issues.

Reader 3

For many reasons, such as the destruction of the land, Haitians rely on imported food. The relative cheapness of imported and donated food also ends up undercutting the ability of local farmers, who lack advanced farming techniques, to compete in their own local market. This causes them to go out of business, and food production falls even more. With rising food and fuel costs, the average Haitian cannot afford enough food for their families each day. Eighty percent of Haitians live in extreme poverty, surviving on just $1 to $2 each day. Many Haitians eat only one meal a day or sometimes no meal at all.

The water quality in Haiti is also very poor, causing many problems including diarrhea, one of the leading causes of deaths in children under 5. Not only is much of the water considered dangerously contaminated for drinking and cooking, it is also often unsafe for bathing, as you can become ill simply through contact with it.

Pray

Pray for a miracle for Haiti's people. Pray for development projects for sustainable water and agriculture. Pray for the leaders of the country to make wise decisions and implement effective solutions to the lack of food and clean water.

Pray that God would provide for and sustain those who are currently suffering.

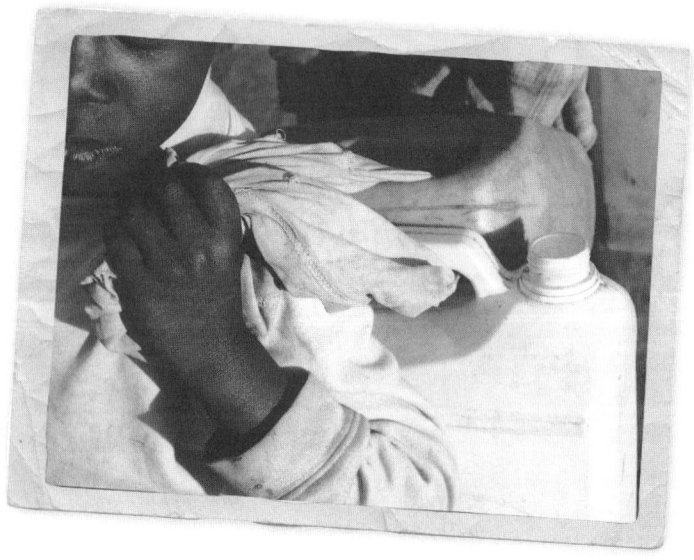

WEEK 4

What the Bible Has to Say

This short Bible study will help you hear God's Word for helping those in need. Moving around your circle or room, have a different person read each numbered portion. If you're in a larger group, form groups of four to six for this section.

Reader 1

Proverbs contains a vast store of practical God-given wisdom and much about how people and countries should treat the poor. Often the writer contrasts God's wisdom with the wisdom (or ignorance) of the wicked. Proverbs 29:7 says, "A righteous man knows the rights of the poor; a wicked man does not understand such knowledge" (English Standard Version).

Discuss

- What "rights" do you think the author is talking about here?
- Where do these rights come from? Why don't the wicked know about them?

Reader 2

The author of Proverbs gives clear indications of what righteousness looks like and its benefits. In Proverbs 22:9, he says, "A generous man will himself be blessed, for he shares his food with the poor."

Discuss

- How do you interpret this verse—as an encouragement, a definition, a promise?
- What do you think "be blessed" means here?

Reader 3

If being blessed isn't enough of a motivation, Proverbs is fairly direct about our need to respond to the rights of the poor. In Proverbs 3:27, it says, "Do not withhold good from those who deserve it, when it is in your power to act."

Discuss

- Who do you tend to think deserves good? How has this opinion been formed in you?
- Who does God say deserves good from us? What are your initial thoughts about this?

Reader 4

James was also very clear about the need to not sit by or only wish the poor well but to deliver to the poor those acts of mercy that we, as the righteous, know are due to them. James 2:17 says, "Faith by itself, if it is not accompanied by action, is dead."

The context of the verses just before verse 17 gives us a very clear picture of what James was actually talking about: "Suppose a brother or sister is without clothes or daily food. If one of you says to him, 'Go, I wish you well; keep warm and well fed,' but does nothing about his physical needs, what good is it?" (James 2:15-16).

Discuss

- How does reading these verses affect how you understand James' words about faith and works?
- Why do you think he chose this, out of all things, as his example?

WEEK 4

Closing

To close your time together, remind people of the noble beginning of Haiti's history as an independent country, and ask them to pray for God's healing hand in this country.

Ideas for Action

- Cut out the Prayer Cards at the end of the book for Week 4, and use these cards to continue praying each day this week for Haiti.

- Through Compassion International, you can sponsor a child from Haiti. This will ensure that he or she has access to school, adequate nutrition, Christian teaching, health checkups, and your love and support. You can also support its Child Survival Program that provides mothers of infants in Haiti with prenatal and postnatal education and access to health care. Visit compassion.com.

Week 5: Prayer for Thailand

"Whoever welcomes one of these little children in my name welcomes me." —Mark 9:37

Hostess Page

Prayer for Thailand

Tropical Thailand is the only Southeast Asian country never to have been colonized. Although its economy is on the rise, it is still plagued by issues such as child trafficking and prostitution.

A Taste of Thailand

Mango Sticky Rice is a very easy (and very tasty) dessert for your gathering. You can prepare the rice ahead of time. (Thanks to Brandy Campbell for the recipe!)

Mango Sticky Rice

Rice
- 1½ cups uncooked short-grain white rice
- 2 cups water
- 1½ cups light coconut milk
- ¾ cup sugar
- ½ teaspoon salt

Coconut Sauce
- ½ cup light coconut milk
- 1 tablespoon sugar
- ¼ teaspoon salt
- 1 tablespoon cornstarch

Toppings
- 3 mangoes, peeled and sliced
- 1 tablespoon toasted sesame seeds (optional)
- toasted coconut (optional)
- coconut ice cream (optional)

Combine rice and water in a saucepan, and bring to a boil. Cover and reduce heat to low. Simmer until all water is absorbed, 15 to 20 minutes. (Or rice can be prepared in a rice cooker). While rice is cooking, combine the coconut milk, sugar, and salt in a saucepan over medium heat. Bring to a boil; then remove from heat. Stir cooked rice into the coconut milk mixture and cover, cooling for 1 hour.

Week 5

To make the coconut sauce, mix the coconut milk, sugar, salt, and cornstarch in a saucepan, and bring to a boil.

Place the sticky rice on a serving dish, and arrange sliced mangoes on top of rice. Pour the sauce over the mangoes and rice. Garnish with sesame seeds and toasted coconut if desired. Serve with coconut ice cream.

Sweet Thai Iced Tea

- black tea
- water
- sweetened condensed milk

Prepare enough black tea for each guest, and refrigerate to chill. Serve over ice, and top each glass with 1 to 2 tablespoons of sweetened condensed milk.

Creating the Thailand Experience

- Teach women the traditional Thai greeting as they arrive. The youngest person presses her hands together with fingertips pointing upwards and bows her head to touch her hands, and says, "Sawat-dii ka." The other then responds in the same way.

- Thailand is a tropical country with jungles and mountains. Decorate your area by bringing in as many leafy green plants as you can find to give it a tropical flair.

- Eat your dessert sitting on the floor, shoes off, in the traditional Thai way of eating.

Week 5

Prayer Stations

For this week's prayer time, you'll set up Prayer Stations around your meeting area. These could be different rooms for a larger group or simply different corners or areas of your room for a smaller group. You can place signs indicating which station is which. Women will use their own copies of this book to prompt them what to do at each station.

You can choose to have women form small groups of four or five to go through the stations or have them move from station to station individually. Cue women when it's time to move from one station to another. Here's what you'll need to do to prepare each station area:

Prayer Station 1: At the first station, women will journal in their Passport to Prayer books. Have pens ready at this station.

Prayer Station 2: At this station, women will use flowers to pray. (See Unforgettable Experience.) Either have a bouquet of flowers here or women's flowers from the Experience waiting for them here.

Prayer Station 3: At this station, women will pray for the church and Christians in Thailand. Have matches and a candle or several candles here for women to light. (If possible, have this station in a dark area.)

Unforgettable Experience

You'll do the Unforgettable Experience after the women have done the Needs and Issues in Thailand section. We'll explain the Experience here—but you'll do it later in your time together. You'll need one flower for each woman, such as a daisy, carnation, or rose.

When you've completed the Needs and Issues in Thailand section, hand a flower to each woman.

Say: Looking at your flower, think of a young girl in your life who is special. It could be your daughter, a niece, a neighbor, a student, or a friend. Think about the things you love about that girl. Looking at the flower, think about how the girl who is special to you is similar to the flower. Pray for these little girls whom God wants to be able to just be children.

Week 5

Share: Have each woman turn to the person sitting next to her and tell how the girl in her life is similar to the flower.

After women have answered, remind them that just like the girls in their lives are special and unique, so are the girls in Thailand, whom God created. However, Thai girls are suffering because of trafficking and sex slavery.

Tell women to trade flowers with their partners. Then tell each woman to take the flower in her hand and smash it, rip the petals off, or destroy it in some way. This may make women mad or upset, but have them do it anyway. As they destroy the flowers, take them through the following discussion:

Say: When these girls, who are so precious to God, are forced into prostitution, part of them is destroyed. When they are still young and delicate, their innocence is taken away, and this is never what God intended for their lives. Just as these delicate flowers are destroyed, these children in Thailand are being horribly damaged.

Ask: How did you feel when your partner destroyed your flower?

Say: Just as you love the little girls in your life, and it angers and shocks you to have a symbol of them destroyed, God loves the children in Thailand who are being destroyed by trafficking and slavery, and he is angry about what is being done to them.

Let's learn what the Bible has to say about these little ones, how we can pray for them, and what we can do.

At this point, you can give each woman a fresh flower to replace the one that was destroyed; or you can give each woman a new flower at the closing of your time as a reminder to pray for the girls in Thailand. After the Unforgettable Experience, transition into your Bible study.

WEEK 5

Learning About Thailand

Thailand Pop Quiz

Take this quiz together to see what you know about Thailand! It's fun to see what everyone knows about distant countries, and this quiz will help everyone get a feel for what this country is like. The answers are on the last page of this chapter. Choose one woman to read the answers.

1. **The country of Thailand is about what size?**
    a. the size of West Virginia
    b. two times the size of Wyoming
    c. the size of Oregon

2. **What religion are the majority of Thai people?**
    a. Christian
    b. Muslim
    c. Buddhist

3. **What did Thailand used to be known as?**
    a. Burma
    b. Bangkok
    c. Siam

4. **Which of these is not true of Thailand?**
    a. Thailand is the world's number one exporter of rice.
    b. Thailand is the number one tourist destination of Southeast Asia.
    c. The national sport of Thailand is cricket.

5. **What are the two largest people groups in Thailand?**
    a. Thai and Chinese
    b. Thai and Malaysian
    c. Thai and Indian

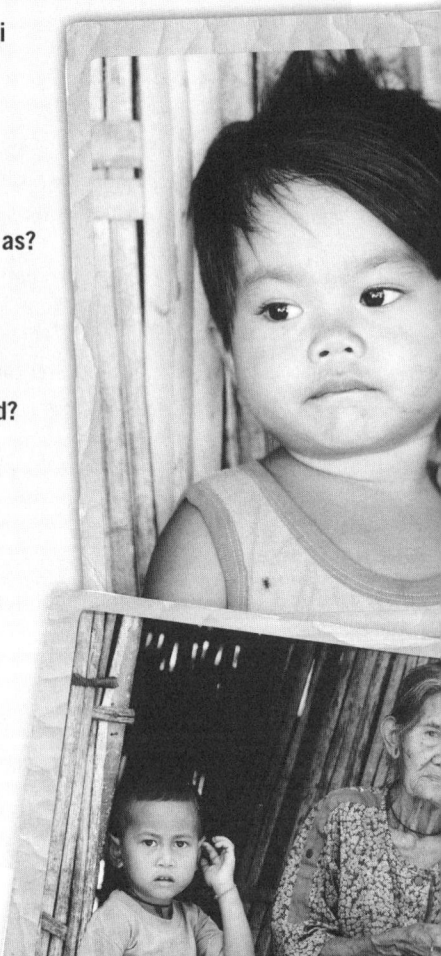

66

Needs and Issues in Thailand

Have a different reader read each issue facing Thailand.

Reader 1
Government Corruption

Thailand has been plagued by corrupt police, military, and government leaders. The corrupt leaders protect and participate in the drug networks, crime syndicates, environmental degradation, and the very large sex trade industry in the country, resulting in human rights violations, bribery, and lack of enforcement of laws to protect citizens.

Reader 2
Drugs

Drug use has long been an issue in Thailand. There has been a drug dependence on opium for centuries, and heroin use has been epidemic at different times in the last century. Thailand is also now a major consumer of methamphetamines, and the country is a transit point for drugs leaving Burma and Laos and a center for money laundering.

The government has staged brutal crackdowns on drugs, which has resulted in human rights violations, including as many as 3,000 deaths without trial, including innocent women and children.

Reader 3
Separatist Insurgency

For many years there has been a separatist insurgency in the south of Thailand, which is predominantly Malaysian. This has resulted in thousands of deaths, the burning of schools, and a series of bomb attacks. The problem and violence have been escalating since 2005.

Reader 4
Spotlight Need: Sex Trafficking

Sex tourism is a thriving industry in Thailand, fueled by the trafficking of people into sex slavery. Around the world the value of illicit human trafficking is estimated to be over $32 billion. Each year more than 2 million children are exploited in the global sex trade.

People from all over the world, especially Westerners, visit Thailand because of the sex industry. Young girls, boys, and women from places like Burma, Laos, and less developed tribes in the north of Thailand are kidnapped or sold into sex slavery at brothels in Bangkok and around the country.

Many of those trafficked are from areas deep in poverty, who are promised jobs as housemaids or hair stylists but instead find themselves in conditions of slavery, forced to act as prostitutes. Government officials and police are complicit in the recruitment and transportation of these children.

Note to Hostess: Remember to do the Unforgettable Experience here.

What the Bible Has to Say

If your group is large, form small groups of four to five for this short Bible study that will help you hear God's Word and God's hope for children in Thailand and guide your prayer. Take about 10 minutes for this so you'll have plenty of time to pray.

Reader 1

Mark 9:37 says, "Whoever welcomes one of these little children in my name welcomes me; and whoever welcomes me does not welcome me but the one who sent me."

Jesus makes a direct correlation between giving kindness to children with giving kindness to himself, and through him directly to God.

Discuss

- How does the world's attitude toward children differ from God's? Why?
- Why do you think God considers children so important or service to them so worthwhile?

Reader 2

Matthew 18:6-7 says, "But if anyone causes one of these little ones who believe in me to sin, it would be better for him to have a large millstone hung around his neck and to be drowned in the depths of the sea. Woe to the world because of the things that cause people to sin! Such things must come, but woe to the man through whom they come!"

Verses 8-9 continue: "If your hand or your foot causes you to sin, cut it off and throw it away. It is better for you to enter life maimed or crippled than to have two hands or two feet and be thrown into eternal fire. And if your eye causes you to sin, gouge it out and throw it away. It is better for you to enter life with one eye than to have two eyes and be thrown into the fire of hell."

In the same way that God considers acts done out of Christian love for a child so important, God considers wrongs done to children equally important.

Discuss

- How does reading these verses change your understanding of how important the treatment of children is to God?
- How does reading verses 8 and 9 in the context of verses 6 and 7 change your understanding of them? Why are these verses so severe?

Reader 3

Matthew 18:2-5 says, "He called a little child and had him stand among them. And he said: 'I tell you the truth, unless you change and become like little children, you will never enter the kingdom of heaven. Therefore, whoever humbles himself like this child is the greatest in the kingdom of heaven. And whoever welcomes a little child like this in my name welcomes me.'"

Verse 10 continues, "See that you do not look down on one of these little ones. For I tell you that their angels in heaven always see the face of my Father in heaven."

Jesus set a new standard for caring about children and their value to God. Learning to care for children is learning to care for what God cares for. With all the important people and things to care about in the world, the angels of the children always see the face of the Father.

Discuss

- Who do you picture as being someone who is close to God and important to God's plans?
- Who should be in your picture, based on what you've read? How do you need to change your attitudes or actions to better fit God's priorities?

WEEK 5

Prayer Time

During this week's prayer time, instead of praying for a number of needs, you'll focus on praying for those who are trafficked into the sex trade and industry in Thailand. Your hostess will have set up various prayer stations before your meeting.

The hostess will guide you in moving through each prayer station. As you go through each station, read through these prompts as you pray.

Prayer Station 1

At this station, you'll sort through some of your feelings on this topic and write out your prayer.

First, write about the emotions you felt during the flower experience.

Write here about the emotions you experienced when learning about this issue.

Now write out your thoughts and prayers to God. Whatever you feel you need to write to God is OK. Write out your response to what you've learned and what your prayer is for these women and children.

Prayer Station 2

At this station, pick up the flower the hostess has left for you or your flower from the earlier experience. Think about the girl who you first associated with your flower.

Pray for God's protection and guidance of the special girl in your life.

Now look at the flower and think about how it's similar to a young girl. Pray for those girls who are currently in a situation of being exploited. Pray for God to protect them and show his love and light to them even in this situation. Pray that they will be rescued out of it.

Now pray for those who are in danger of being exploited. Pray that parents, neighbors, and the community will make choices to protect them. Pray for radical change in the government so these children's protection will become a priority.

Now pray for those who have been rescued from this situation. Pray that they would be able to be reintegrated into society and that they would get the counseling and help they need.

Prayer Station 3

At this station, you'll pray for the church and Christians in Thailand.

Think about how the church and Christians can be a light in the darkness of this situation. Light one of the candles at this station.

Pray that God would use the small church in Thailand to be a voice to speak up for these children.

Pray for the Holy Spirit to use the church in Thailand so many will turn to Christ and so their culture will be transformed to be one that speaks out against and stops this kind of abuse.

Pray that God would place and use loving Christian adults in the lives of those who have been rescued from this situation so that they may learn about Christ's love and healing for their pain.

(Before leaving this station, blow out your candle for the next person to light.)

WEEK 5

Closing

Once women have had a chance to go through each station, close your evening by reminding women to cut out the Prayer Cards at the end of the book to continue praying the rest of the week. Give each woman a new flower to take home with her to remind her to pray for the girls in need of protection in Thailand. Remind them that God is strong and can offer hope in a dark world.

Ideas for Action

- Cut out the Prayer Cards for Thailand at the end of the book to keep praying throughout the week.

- Learn more about the issues of human trafficking and how you can help by visiting International Justice Mission at ijm.org.

- Learn more about how to become an abolitionist to end modern-day slavery at love146.org (formerly Justice for Children International).

Thailand Pop Quiz Answers

1. b. Thailand is more than twice as large as Wyoming, with a population of over 65 million people.

2. c. Thailand is almost 95% Buddhist; 5% are Muslim, and 0.7% are Christian.

3. c. Thailand was known as Siam until 1939, and it is the only Southeast Asian country that was never colonized. Bangkok is the capital of Thailand. Thailand shares a border with the country of Burma, or Myanmar.

4. c. is false. The national sport of Thailand is Thai boxing.

5. a. 75% of the people in Thailand are Thai, and 14% are Chinese. The Chinese play a large role in the local economy and control most of the wealth, which is sometimes resented by the Thais.

Week 6: Prayer for Bolivia

"Speak up for those who cannot speak for themselves, for the rights of all who are destitute. Speak up and judge fairly; defend the rights of the poor and needy." —Proverbs 31:8-9

Hostess Page

Prayer for Bolivia

Bolivia is a landlocked country in South America that is about one-and-a-half times the size of Texas. Though it has many natural resources and spans a diverse area ranging from steamy jungles to towering mountains and deserts, it is the poorest country in South America.

A Taste of Bolivia

Bolivian cuisine includes a lot of meat and potatoes. In the lower elevations of Bolivia, a lot of fruit is grown. For an easy snack, serve star fruit and papaya. Or try this traditional Bolivian dessert that tastes like coconut macaroon candy. Bolivians eat it on special occasions.

Cocadas

- 2⅔ cups sweetened shredded coconut
- ¾ cup sweetened condensed milk
- 1 egg
- ½ teaspoon almond extract

In a bowl, mix the coconut, egg, condensed milk, and almond extract. Let it stand for a couple of minutes. Cover the bottom of a baking sheet with parchment paper, and drop the mixture by teaspoons on the sheet. Bake at 325 degrees for 25 minutes or until golden and dry. Makes 24 candies.

Week 6

Creating the Bolivian Experience

More than half of Bolivia's population is made up of the native Quechua and Aymara peoples, whose ancient and colorful cultures have a rich tradition of art, textiles, folklore, and unique music. The Carnaval de Oruro is the biggest cultural event in Bolivia and is considered one of the masterpieces of human cultural heritage. You may not be able to pull off a procession of 28,000 dancers and 10,000 musicians marching for twenty hours through your home, but you can capture a few of the festive details that make this Andean celebration so exciting.

- For genuine Bolivian music, go to boliviaweb.com/radio and follow the directions to listen online. Then keep this radio station streaming at your get-together.

- Hats are big in Bolivia; they're a traditional part of Bolivian dress, including bowlers, fedoras, and broad-rimmed straw hats. Ask your friends to come wearing hats!

- Woven textiles are a rich part of Bolivian history. If you have any bright-colored rugs or blankets, cover your floor and chair backs for added color. Bolivia's textile patterns look similar to Native American patterns but with brighter colors such as fuchsia and yellow.

Unforgettable Experience

Many children in Bolivia live in abject poverty and also suffer child abuse. For your experience together, create Christmas gift boxes to make these children feel special and loved. Go to "Operation Christmas Child" on samaritanspurse.org to find out how to create gift boxes, which you can send to them year-round.

Before your get-together, give your guests a list of ideas for small items they can bring to put into the gift boxes. (You can find out what to put in the boxes at their website.) Then at your meeting, you can put the items together in the boxes and wrap the boxes (wrapping the lids separate from the boxes). Take time to pray for the child who will receive each box, asking God to protect and provide for him or her.

WEEK 6

Learning About and Praying for Bolivia

Read through these pages together, having a different friend read the text of each section. Pause to pray after each prompt, as you learn more about Bolivia. You can have one person pray for each need, or leave it open for "popcorn" prayers.

Reader 1
About Bolivia

Population: about 9.2 million

Religion: 95% of the population is Roman Catholic, and the remaining 5% is primarily Protestant.

Bolivia's culture began with the pre-Columbian peoples, who still make up most of the modern population. Much of that culture remains intact, despite the Spanish colonization and domination by the European minority.

Though Bolivia possesses a wealth of natural resources like metals and natural gas, the country has long been crippled by instability. Since its independence in 1825, it has suffered from a series of almost 200 coups and countercoups. The last 25 years have been much more stable, though, and in 2005 Bolivia elected its first indigenous president, Evo Morales. Tensions have increased since his election, however, bringing racial and economic differences between different regions to the forefront.

Though a very beautiful and diverse country, Bolivia is the third largest producer of coca, a native plant that is the basis for cocaine; and much of Bolivia's population is underemployed and lives in poverty.

Reader 2
Spotlight Need: Protecting and Caring for the Children of Bolivia

Latin America is one of the most violent regions in the world, and children and women are the most common victims. Violence against children is a very serious concern in Bolivia. It's especially important because nearly half the population of the country is made up of children and adolescents. Children are often considered as being the property of their parents rather than as persons of their own with rights, and it is not considered unusual to hit or beat a child to discipline them. As the Violence Against Children Report states, children are at serious risk of extrajudicial executions, torture, inhuman or degrading punishment, corporal punishment, sexual abuse and exploitation, and human trafficking.

Pray

Pause to pray about putting an end to the violence against children in Bolivia. Pray that the Holy Spirit would use the church in Bolivia to transform the culture of violence against children and that children's advocacy groups in Bolivia would be effective in impacting the culture and creating laws to protect the rights of children. Pray that God would comfort, protect, and provide for children who are currently suffering.

Reader 3

Children in Bolivia are subject to a number of problems that endanger their chance for a normal childhood. Because economic conditions are so difficult for many families—roughly 2.5 million children in Bolivia are living in conditions of poverty and extreme poverty (almost a third of the total population of the country)—large numbers of children are forced to work to help keep their families afloat. Of those more than 800,000 children that have to work, less than half continue going to school, making it even harder for them to break out of the cycle of poverty. There is also a growing number of street children in big cities, with no one to care for them.

Pray

Pray for the children in Bolivia who are laborers, are in danger of being trafficked as laborers, and do not have an opportunity for education. Pray for laws to protect child laborers. Pray for a transformation of families in Bolivia so that parents would advocate for their children. Pray also for stability so this resource-rich country can gain economic and investment opportunities to alleviate the country's poverty.

Reader 4

Poverty also threatens the lives of the children of Bolivia. The major causes of death for children up to age 5 (such as diarrhea and malnutrition) are directly related to poverty. And even though mortality rates have been brought down in recent years in Bolivia, they are still very high, and life expectancy is low. More than a quarter of Bolivian children suffer from moderate to severe stunting as a result of malnutrition.

Pray

Pray for education for mothers to learn how to keep their children healthy. Pray for economic opportunity for the families who struggle to feed their children each day.

Reader 5

Children are also threatened by the drug trade, who consider them expendable and use them as packers, couriers, and dealers. It is also not unusual for young men, boys as young as 14, to join or be conscripted into the military. Although the minimum age for performing military service is 18, it is estimated that almost half of the Bolivian armed forces are under 18 years.

Pray

Pray for the protection of the children who would be exploited by the drug trade. Pray that the church would be a safe place for children who might otherwise be attracted to gangs. Pray that the Holy Spirit would transform and heal this country and protect the children.

WEEK 6

What the Bible Has to Say

If your group is large, form small groups of four to five for this short Bible study that will help you hear God's Word and guide your prayer.

Reader 1

Psalm 140:12 says, "I know that the Lord secures justice for the poor and upholds the cause of the needy." No one is more vulnerable and at risk from the consequences of poverty and injustice than children.

In many countries the people have no way of defending themselves and are at the mercy of a culture that doesn't defend them from violence or exploitation. Much of this exploitation isn't even seen or known about. But God calls Christians to an active role in defending the needy. Leviticus 19:16 commands, "Do not stand idly by when your neighbor's life is threatened" (New Living Translation). Ephesians 5:11 says, "Have nothing to do with the fruitless deeds of darkness, but rather expose them."

Discuss

- Do you consider upholding the cause of the needy as more of a defensive or an offensive pursuit? Explain your thoughts.
- How do you think God sees it?

Reader 2

In Isaiah 1:17, God gives a very exacting description of how righteous people should behave and it's often repeated in the Bible: "Seek justice, encourage the oppressed. Defend the cause of the fatherless, plead the case of the widow."

Proverbs 31:8-9 reminds us again of exactly what we should do: "Speak up for those who cannot speak for themselves, for the rights of all who are destitute. Speak up and judge fairly; defend the rights of the poor and needy."

- How have you actively pursued these commands in your life?

- How could you begin to pursue these commands? Be specific.

- How has your understanding of your answer and of these commands changed in light of what you've learned during this study?

Reader 3

God has also said he will bless those who care for the weak and vulnerable, such as children. And his promises aren't small ones but big ones. Psalm 41:1 says, "Blessed is he who has regard for the weak; the Lord delivers him in times of trouble."

Matthew 10:42 says that "If anyone gives even a cup of cold water to one of these little ones because he is my disciple, I tell you the truth, he will certainly not lose his reward."

Reader 4

Giving care to the children of the world because of God's love also promises a brighter future for those who receive it. Proverbs 22:6 says, "Train a child in the way he should go, and when he is old he will not turn from it." Psalm 27:10 also reminds us that even if the whole culture is broken, God is their ultimate hope and can rescue and provide them with all they need: "Though my father and mother forsake me, the Lord will receive me."

Discuss

If the children of a nation such as Bolivia could be brought up to know and reflect God's love, how do you think it would transform the country?

Write

"Speak up for those who cannot speak for themselves, for the rights of all who are destitute. Speak up and judge fairly; defend the rights of the poor and needy."
(Proverbs 31:8-9)

Write here your prayer to God regarding this verse. If you haven't considered how you can speak up for those in need, ask God how you can. If you're scared or intimidated by this verse, write that. Write your honest prayer to God about this verse.

WEEK 6

Closing

After everyone has had a chance to write, close your time together with prayer, appealing to God for the safety and health of the children of Bolivia.

Ideas for Action

- Take a Virtual Field Trip. If you want to learn more about the country of Bolivia and its needs, you can take a virtual field trip there on CARE Bolivia's website. This will help you better understand and appreciate this beautiful but struggling country. Visit care.org/vft/bolivia.

- There are numerous organizations that seek to improve conditions for children in Bolivia. CARE Bolivia, Compassion International, SOS Children's Villages, and Christian Children's Fund all do important work protecting and caring for the young of the nation and striving to provide them with safe and happy homes.

Week 7: Prayer for Afghanistan

"In fact, everyone who wants to live a godly life in Christ Jesus will be persecuted." — 2 Timothy 3:12

Hostess Page

Prayer for Afghanistan

Afghanistan is a rugged land of spectacular mountains that sits at the crossroads of Asia, Europe, and the Middle East. A succession of armies and migrations sweeping across it through the centuries has created a diverse culture with no ethnic majority. Its history and forbidding geography have also made it hard to find peace and unity, something Afghans are fighting for every day now in the wake of Afghanistan's first democratically elected president.

A Taste of Afghanistan

Fresh and dried fruits and nuts are key parts of Afghan cuisine. They produce grapes, apricots, pomegranates, melons, plums, berries, oranges, walnuts, almonds, pistachios, and pine nuts.

For a tasty, authentic Afghan snack, serve dried apricots and almonds and pistachios and grapes with some tea. Or try this tasty snack, similar to baklava, a popular Middle Eastern dessert.

Asabia el Aroos (Bride's Fingers)

- half of a 16-ounce package of phyllo dough, thawed
- ¼ cup melted butter
- ½ cup almonds
- ⅓ cup sugar, plus extra to sprinkle on top
- 1 egg, beaten

To make filling, finely chop the almonds in a food processor and mix in ⅓ cup sugar. Cut the phyllo dough in half crosswise and in half again. Lay two of the rectangles stacked in front of you, with shorter sides toward you. (Cover remaining dough with a dampened towel.) Brush with butter. Put a tablespoon of filling in a line across the shorter side.

Week 7

Asabia el Aroos (Bride's Fingers) cont.

Fold in edges, and then roll up like a cigar. Repeat with remaining dough and filling. Brush with the beaten egg, and sprinkle with sugar. Bake at 375 degrees for 15 to 20 minutes or until browned.

Creating the Afghan Experience

See the Unforgettable Experience for ways you can create the experience of many Afghan Christians.

Unforgettable Experience

In a country of nearly 33 million people, there are only 500 to 10,000 Christians. The exact numbers are difficult to know because most Christians keep their faith hidden. (Not one Christian church building exists.) Many people of minority faiths, such as Jewish, Christian, and Bahai, fled during the Taliban's rule. Since then, although the Afghan constitution technically allows religious freedom, Christians still face severe persecution, including death, from their neighbors. If anyone finds out you're a Christian, you have a choice to either flee the country or likely be killed.

Week 7

For your get-together, help your friends experience what it might be like for those Afghan Christians who have to hide their faith. Here are some ideas to create the evening:

- When arriving, ask women to not all park in front of your house or meeting area. Ask them to park around the block and walk to the meeting so there are not a lot of cars in one spot.

- Ask women to make sure nothing on their persons would show that they're going to a Christian meeting. If they bring a Bible, ask them to hide it inside their clothing or put a book cover on it.

- Have women enter through a door that isn't very visible to neighbors (for example, a back or side door).

- Inside your meeting, have all the blinds or shades closed to cover the windows.

- Ask one person to be your lookout during the meeting, guarding the door.

- Be discreet during the meeting—dim lights and talk in low voices.

- Be prepared to hide your Bibles so that if anyone walked in, it would look like just another social gathering.

- Before this meeting, tell your friends to consider whether or not they are willing to come to the meeting—knowing that if they come and anyone finds out about it, they'll either have to flee the country or face severe persecution—even death.

Note: Be sure to read the Hostess section for the following week before you meet for this week. There are things you'll need to mention at the end of this meeting so women will be prepared for next week.

WEEK 7

Learning About and Praying for Afghanistan

Afghanistan Pop Quiz

Take this quiz together to see what you know about Afghanistan! It's fun to see what everyone knows about distant countries, and this quiz will help everyone get a feel for what this country is like. The answers are on the last page of this week's study. Choose one woman to read the answers.

1. Which of these countries does Afghanistan not share a border with?
    a. Iran
    b. Pakistan
    c. Nepal
    d. China

2. Which of these historic peoples occupied or invaded Afghanistan?
    a. The Persians, Alexander the Great's Greeks, and the Greco-Bactrians
    b. The Parthians, Genghis Khan's Mongols, and the Russians
    c. The Huns, the Kushans, and the Turks
    d. All of the above

3. What is the elevation of the highest point in Afghanistan?

4. Afghanistan is the world's largest producer of what crop?

5. Afghanistan is about the same size as what state?
    a. Wyoming
    b. Texas
    c. Georgia
    d. California

WEEK 7

Prayer Time

Read through this section together, having a different friend read each portion. As you learn more about Afghanistan, pause to pray after each prompt.

Reader 1
The Results of Years of War and Instability

Afghanistan has been in a state of perpetual upheaval and emergency for the last three decades. After the withdrawal of the Soviets, the country descended into a state of civil war. Eventually the oppressive Taliban regime emerged victorious but was overthrown in 2001 by a U.S.-aided coalition. These long years of conflict have left much of the essential infrastructure of the country in ruins. Major services such as basic education, health care, and transportation are being rebuilt from the ground up. Because of the limited reach of the government and the rule of law, though, many of its provinces are still very unstable and dangerous.

Reader 2

Afghanistan is groaning from the mass of troubles these years of conflict and wholesale destruction have visited on them. Forty percent of the population is unemployed. Overgrazing, soil degradation, and deforestation are rampant. Twenty-five percent of all Afghan children die before reaching their fifth birthday, and 50 women die every day from pregnancy-related complications. Approximately 200,000 Afghans have been disabled by exploding mines left over from the wars, and the number climbs every month. Life expectancy is only 44 years.

Afghanistan has a wealth of mineral resources, but without the necessary stability, infrastructure, and foreign investment, it has been virtually unable to exploit them. Agriculture and industry methods are essentially premodern and, in some cases, primitive. The country has no functioning railways and no highways. Government authority is growing, but the country is still terribly divided.

Pray

Pray for peace, stability, and unity in Afghanistan. Pray for investment and development in the country so that infrastructure can be built. Pray for the development of the educational system so that skilled workers can be trained.

Reader 3
The Drug Trade

The opium trade in Afghanistan is unprecedented in the history of the world. Not only is it the world's largest producer of opium but opium accounts for nearly a third of the entire country's gross domestic product. An enormous percentage of the population is involved in opium production, and much of the revenue that supplies the anti-government insurgency comes from the illegal drug trade. Because it is so pervasive, the trade is terribly difficult to fight, as so many people rely on it for their means of survival, and there is so much widespread corruption and lawlessness.

Pray

Pray for the end of the drug trade. Pray for legitimate work for the workers to transfer to, and leaders to fight government corruption. Pray for the restoration of other crops. Pray for the trade to switch to legal trade, such as trade in medicinal morphine.

Reader 4
Oppression of Women and Human Rights Violations

Afghanistan has a history of terrible human rights violations going back to the Soviet invasion in 1979. Mass killings, torture, lawless arrests, and oppression left scars on the country that were only made worse in the following civil war. When the Taliban came to power, it specifically targeted women as the objects of its persecution, justifying its actions with fundamentalist Islamic law.

Reader 5

During this period, all women were essentially under house arrest, unable to leave home or seek medical care without a male escort, unable to attend school, unable to work outside the home, unable to appear in public unless wearing a complete body covering with only a mesh screen to see and breathe through, and even unable to wear shoes that made noise when they walked. An estimate in the year 2000 stated that less than 13% of Afghan women could read and write.

Recovery from this disastrous regime has been slow, and though things are much better now, women still face enormous challenges and prejudice, especially when it comes to education. The need for women teachers is especially great.

Pray

Thank God for the lessening of the burden on women after the ousting of the Taliban.

Pray for a transformation of the culture that oppresses women. Pray for education for women and girls. Pray for women teachers and leaders to be raised up and just laws to be put in place to protect women.

Reader 6
Food Insecurity

Over the last decade, Afghanistan has suffered through periods of devastating drought as well as earthquakes, flash floods, and suffocating snows. Armed conflict as well as natural disasters have driven down agriculture to the point where the country can no longer grow enough food to feed its population. About 70% of the population lives in poverty or substandard conditions, 40% of children under three are underweight, and more than half of the children under five are stunted as a result of poor nutrition. It is also very difficult for aid agencies to help those in need, as the neediest places are also unsafe and hard to access as a result of blocked or ruined roads and anti-government insurgencies.

Pray

Pray for the healing of their land, that Afghanistan's subsistence farmers would be able to grow enough to feed their families. Pray for education in good agricultural practices. Pray for the children who are not getting enough food to become healthy, thriving adults. Pray for aid agencies to have access to help those who are suffering the most.

Reader 7
Christians and Religious Persecution

Under the Taliban, intense persecution of non-Muslims and Shi'a Muslims existed. Many people of the religious minority have fled. Since the Taliban's fall, the Afghanistan constitution technically allows religious freedom, but there is still much persecution. Not one church building exists, and few Christians survive in this hostile environment. It's hard to know the exact number because most are not open with their faith. Afghanistan is still one of the least-reached countries in the world, with many people groups never having heard the gospel.

Pray

Pray for the strengthening and empowerment of the Christians in Afghanistan. Pray that they would become mature followers of Christ. Pray for their protection against persecution. Pray for the millions in Afghanistan who have never had an opportunity to hear the gospel.

WEEK 7

What the Bible Has to Say

If your group is large, form small groups of four to five for this short Bible study that will help you hear God's Word and God's hope for Afghanistan and guide your prayer.

Reader 1

The Bible makes it plain that persecution is a guaranteed outcome of following Christ. 2 Timothy 3:12 says, "In fact, everyone who wants to live a godly life in Christ Jesus will be persecuted."

Discuss

- Is persecution something you expect in your life? Why or why not?
- Tell about your own experiences with persecution.

Reader 2

Christians in different places may experience different amounts and kinds of persecution. The Apostle Paul gives good guidance on how those of us fortunate to live in safe, prosperous countries should conduct ourselves. Colossians 4:2-6 says, "Devote yourselves to prayer, being watchful and thankful. And pray for us, too, that God may open a door for our message, so that we may proclaim the mystery of Christ, for which I am in chains. Pray that I may proclaim it clearly, as I should. Be wise in the way you act toward outsiders; make the most of every opportunity. Let your conversation be always full of grace, seasoned with salt, so that you may know how to answer everyone."

Discuss

As God has placed you in a place relatively free of religious persecution, what do you think your role should be?

Reader 3

The Bible reminds us that our hope for all Christians for freedom and safety is in God, not in governments or armies or laws or organizations. Second Corinthians 4:6-9 says, "For God, who said, 'Let light shine out of darkness,' made his light shine in our hearts to give us the light of the knowledge of the glory of God in the face of Christ. But we have this treasure in jars of clay to show that this all-surpassing power is from God and not from us. We are hard pressed on every side, but not crushed; perplexed, but not in despair; persecuted, but not abandoned; struck down, but not destroyed."

Discuss

- What are the risks of putting our hope in achieving strength and security through worldly means?
- What hope does this give you for the power of prayer?

Reader 4

Our hope is in God, and God has chosen to give us a truly important part in empowering Christians, both those at home and those persecuted abroad, through prayer. Ephesians 6:18 says, "And pray in the Spirit on all occasions with all kinds of prayers and requests. With this in mind, be alert and always keep on praying for all the saints."

Discuss

What can you do to keep the needs of Christians worldwide and your role in helping them clear in your mind? Be specific.

WEEK 7

Closing

To close your evening, remind your friends that you are meeting in secrecy. Ask them to leave the event one by one, quietly and at staggered intervals, so that the group will be unobtrusive.

Ideas for Action

- If you want to stay informed about the persecution of Christians around the world, sign up for Voice of the Martyrs newsletter at persecution.org.

- Read *Three Cups of Tea*, a book about one man's work to bring education to children, especially girls, in Pakistan and Afghanistan, or learn more about how you can get involved in providing Afghan girls with education at threecupsoftea.com.

- If you want to learn more about Afghanistan and how you can help Afghanistan's children, go to unicef.org.

Afghanistan Pop Quiz Answers

1. c. Nepal.

2. d. All of the above. But those are just some of the ones who have invaded and occupied Afghanistan. The Silk Road, the trade route between Asia and Europe, runs through it, making it a major target for conquest.

3. Noshaq Mountain is 24,557 feet. (For a point of reference, the highest point in the continental U.S. is Mount Whitney, at 14,505 feet, 10,000 feet lower than Noshaq.

4. Opium. Most of the heroin consumed in Europe and Eurasia is derived from Afghan poppies.

5. b. Texas.

Week 8: Prayer for Vision

"For we are God's workmanship, created in Christ Jesus to do good works, which God prepared in advance for us to do." —Ephesians 2:10

Hostess Page

Prayer for Vision

This last week of your study, you'll reflect on how God has challenged you and changed you, and ask God to reveal to you what he has next for you.

A Taste of the World

As it's the last week of this study, consider sharing a meal to celebrate your time together. Consider having an international feast, with each person bringing a dish from the country she was most intrigued by or interested in. Or each woman could bring a dish from a country she would like to learn more about (and pray for).

Tell your guests in Week 7 that in Week 8 they'll consider if there is one area or issue or act that they feel God is calling them to learn more about so they can start thinking about it before this meeting. If they want, they could even do some research on that particular topic to prepare before coming this week. Then each person can bring a dish from the country they were most intrigued or challenged by.

During your meal, have each woman tell about what she brought and why, and what has challenged and surprised her over the past weeks.

Unforgettable Experience

It's easy to feel like one person is too small to do very much to change the world or help others. This fun experiment will remind you how much just a small amount of faith can do.

You'll need one pack of Mentos and one 2-liter bottle of Diet Coke. Do this experience outside or someplace easy to clean up…it might get messy.

Week 8

Say: It's easy to feel overwhelmed by the needs in the world because it doesn't seem like one person's actions or one person's prayers could really do much to help.

But in Matthew 17:20, Jesus says, "I tell you the truth, if you have faith as small as a mustard seed, you can say to this mountain, 'Move from here to there' and it will move. Nothing will be impossible for you."

Let's do an experiment to see how something small can have a big impact.

Then follow these steps:

- Open the bottle of soda, and place it on the ground where it won't tip over.

- Have guests stand back.

- Unwrap the roll of Mentos. (You'll drop all the candies in at once, so it helps to roll a piece of paper into a tube around the Mentos so you can plop them in at once.)

- Drop all the Mentos into the bottle of Coke at once.

- You might want to run away from the soda now…

Watch what happens! You can have a couple of extra bottles and rolls of candies ready in case your audience would like an encore. Once you've cleaned up, ask:

- Tell about examples of someone you've heard of or know who made a big impact on someone else or on the world around them?

- Is it easy or hard for you to believe that your faith and prayer can "move mountains"? Explain your thoughts about this.

- If you or your faith is the Mentos, what do you want the Diet Coke geyser in your life to be? What one mountain would you like to see moved?

WEEK 8

What the Bible Has to Say

Pray

After the Mentos experiment, open with a prayer that God will fill each of you with his Holy Spirit and open your ears to hear his voice as you seek his vision for you.

> *Discuss*
>
> What's the biggest way you've been challenged or changed during the past eight weeks?

Moving around your circle or room, have a different person read each numbered part. If you're in a larger group, you may want to form groups of four to six for this section.

Reader 1

"For we are God's workmanship, created in Christ Jesus to do good works, which God prepared in advance for us to do" (Ephesians 2:10).

It's easy to feel powerless when we look at the world full of needs, but God prepared good works in advance for each of us to do.

> *Discuss*
>
> So far, what do you think some of the good works are that God prepared for you to do in your life? How do you think you've done in these?

Reader 2

In serving others, God wants us to use the gifts he's given us to help others.

1 Peter 4:10-11 says, "Each one should use whatever gift he has received to serve others, faithfully administering God's grace in its various forms. If anyone speaks, he should do it as one speaking the very words of God. If anyone serves, he should do it with the strength God provides, so that in all things God may be praised through Jesus Christ."

Discuss

- What are some of the different gifts God gives people to serve others? (If you need some help, look up Ephesians 4:11-13; Romans 12:6-8; 1 Corinthians 12:7-10, 27-28.)
- What gifts do you think God has given you to serve others? How are you currently using those?

Reader 3

God created each person differently to serve others in a unique way. Although not each one of us is created to respond to each need in the world, God does have specific good works he's prepared for each one of us.

Discuss

- What's grabbed your heart during the past eight weeks? Is there a particular need, a particular country, or a particular act (such as prayer, fasting, or giving) that you think God might want you to do? (It's OK if the answer doesn't have to do with this study!)
- What are ways you might use the way God has gifted you to act in faith to respond in this particular area? Be specific.

Reflecting, Praying, and Journaling

It's so important to seek God's direction for the good works he has in store for us.

For this section you'll need a pen. Move away from each other—even to different rooms or outside, if possible—so everyone can have a personal time of reflecting, praying, and journaling. Decide together a specific time to meet back, allowing a minimum of 15 minutes for this. Longer is better if you have the time!

Pray

Pray to God, asking him to fill you with his Holy Spirit, and ask him to guide you in this time of seeking what good works he might have prepared for you to do.

Write

What did you learn or experience during this study that surprised you?

What one thing affected you the most during this study?

Is there any particular issue or people or action that God is laying on your heart? This might be a desire to pray or fast more or a desire to learn more about a particular issue; it might be a desire to do something in response to something you've learned; or it might be something completely different altogether.

Pray

Tell God that you want to use the gifts he's given you to serve others.

Lay at his feet what you just wrote about. (You might even set this book down on the ground as a symbol of this as you pray.) Ask that his Holy Spirit would guide you and give you direction in how to help and serve others.

Write

- What gifts do you think God has given you to serve others?

- Is there some way you can use these particular gifts to respond to what you feel God is giving you a heart for?

Pray

Lay what you wrote at God's feet.

Ask God that he would use you. Ask if there is a particular way he wants you to use your gifts to serve others.

Write your thoughts or prayers here. Ask God for his guidance.

Commit what you've written and prayed about to God. Then write down one step you're going to take in the next week—whether it be to pray for God's direction, do some research, or talk to someone about what you wrote.

Closing

After the allotted amount of time has passed, join with the rest of your group. (If you're in a large group, you might want to do these next steps in pairs or groups of three.)

- Take time to share with others in your group what you thought or prayed about. Share as much as you are comfortable sharing.
- Share what your next step is in seeking God's direction for what he might have next for you.
- Turn to "Week 8: My Prayer" on page 113. Take time now to fill out this page and sign it.
- Once you've each written your prayer, close your time together in prayer. Place your hand on your commitment as you pray. Thank God for all he's done in the past eight weeks. Ask him for his continued direction as you seek to serve him.

Cut out these cards to help you pray each day this week.

Week 1: Prayer for the World

"But you, dear friends, build yourselves up in your most holy faith and pray in the Holy Spirit" (Jude 1:20).

"In this world you will have trouble. But take heart! I have overcome the world" (John 16:33).

"Looking at his disciples, he said: 'Blessed are you who are poor, for yours is the kingdom of God. Blessed are you who hunger now, for you will be satisfied. Blessed are you who weep now, for you will laugh' "—(Luke 6:20-21).

"The apostles said to the Lord, 'Increase our faith!' He replied, 'If you have faith as small as a mustard seed, you can say to this mulberry tree, "Be uprooted and planted in the sea," and it will obey you'" (Luke 17:5-6).

"And pray in the Spirit on all occasions with all kinds of prayers and requests. With this in mind, be alert and always keep on praying for all the saints" (Ephesians 6:18).

"And whatever you do, whether in word or deed, do it all in the name of the Lord Jesus, giving thanks to God the Father through him" (Colossians 3:17).

Week 1: Prayer for the World

Pray that God would fill you with his Holy Spirit as you pray for others and that in these next eight weeks, you would be praying in his will and through his strength and not your own.

Pray that you wouldn't become overwhelmed as you learn about the needs in the world and that God would help you take heart in knowing that Christ has overcome this world. Pray that God would give you his peace and his love for this world.

Pray that God would increase your faith and that you would believe in his power to "demolish strongholds" in this world of need through your prayers.

Pray that God will help you view the poor, those who are weak and in need, the way he views them—as his blessed creation. Pray that God would help you have the attitude that he has for those in need.

Commit the next eight weeks to God, asking that he would use this study to change you and the world around you.

Pray that God would give you strength and lasting passion through his Holy Spirit to pray continually for others. Pray that God would help you be alert and always keep on praying.

Week 2: Prayer for Uganda

Malaria
One in six Ugandan children die of malaria, and the high incidence of malaria keeps many adults from working consistently and children from attending school.

Political Stability and Recovery
There has been much political instability in the past several decades in Uganda, and there are 1.27 million internally displaced persons in Uganda.

AIDS
Since 1982, 2.6 million Ugandans have been diagnosed with AIDS and 1.6 million have died, leaving nearly 1 million orphans in Uganda.

Vulnerable Children
AIDS has left a large number of orphans and street children in Uganda. Approximately 25,000 children have also been kidnapped to serve as child soldiers or as sex slaves during wartime.

The Church
Uganda's population is 42% Protestant, and another 42% is Catholic; 12% is Muslim.

Food Insecurity
With rising fuel and food prices, it becomes difficult for those living in poverty to afford even their daily meals. In some places, agricultural practices that aren't environmentally sustainable are used. Natural disasters, such as heavy rains or drought, can also destroy crops each year.

Week 2: Prayer for Uganda

Pray for a final and lasting peace in Uganda. Pray for a government that shuns corruption and puts the good of its people first. Pray that those displaced would be able to safely return home and become self-supporting. Pray that the children displaced by war would have access to health care and education through the help of the government and aid organizations.

Pray for effective malaria prevention—that the government and other organizations would be able to effectively educate on malaria prevention and get funds to distribute bed nets. Pray for the relief and comfort of those who are suffering from malaria.

Pray for the spiritual, emotional, physical, and social welfare of the highly vulnerable children in Uganda. Pray that God would place responsible and caring adults in their lives, and they would be integrated back into society.

Pray for effective education and prevention of AIDS. Pray for the government and nonprofit organizations to make wise decisions about how to address the issue. Pray for those who have AIDS and are suffering discrimination. Pray for the orphans AIDS has left behind.

Pray that sustainable agricultural practices would be used among farmers. Pray for the success of small-scale agricultural ventures for subsistence farmers. Pray for a long-term solution to the global rising cost of fuel and food.

Pray for the unity of the Ugandan church between denominations and tribes. Pray that the churches would rely on God's strength and the Holy Spirit. Pray that the church would be able to respond to the needs of its country. Pray that Ugandan Christians would be able to share the good news of God's grace with their Muslim neighbors.

Week 3: Prayer for India

"We always thank God for all of you, mentioning you in our prayers. We continually remember before our God and Father your work produced by faith, your labor prompted by love, and your endurance inspired by hope in our Lord Jesus Christ" (1 Thessalonians 1:2-3).

"[Jesus] told them, 'The harvest is plentiful, but the workers are few. Ask the Lord of the harvest, therefore, to send out workers into his harvest field'" (Luke 10:2).

"We ought always to thank God for you... because your faith is growing more and more, and the love every one of you has for each other is increasing. Therefore, among God's churches we boast about your perseverance and faith in all the persecutions and trials you are enduring. All this is evidence that God's judgment is right, and as a result you will be counted worthy of the kingdom of God, for which you are suffering" (2 Thessalonians 1:3-5).

"And if anyone causes one of these little ones who believe in me to sin, it would be better for him to be thrown into the sea with a large millstone tied around his neck" (Mark 9:42).

"He will defend the afflicted among the people and save the children of the needy; he will crush the oppressor" (Psalm 72:4).

"When they cry out to the Lord because of their oppressors, he will send them a savior and defender, and he will rescue them" (Isaiah 19:20).

Week 3: Prayer for India

Pray for those in India who have never heard of Jesus, that God would raise up workers.

Praise God for the Indian church—its leaders, preachers, writers, and apologists. Thank God for the church across India that is growing in unity and maturity through persecution.

Pray for children who need protection from abusers and those who would exploit them, that they would find shelter and comfort in God and help from trusted adults.

Pray for the protection and strength of those who are being persecuted for their faith.

Pray that girls will be treated with respect and dignity and value. Pray for a transformed society that values all people through the power of the Holy Spirit.

Pray for those trapped in poverty, that God would provide for their needs, raise up leaders to eradicate poverty, and break the cycle of poverty.

Week 4: Prayer for Haiti

"And if you spend yourselves in behalf of the hungry and satisfy the needs of the oppressed, then your light will rise in the darkness, and your night will become like the noonday" (Isaiah 58:10).

"Rich and poor have this in common: The Lord is the Maker of them all" (Proverbs 22:2).

"Speak up for those who cannot speak for themselves, for the rights of all who are destitute. Speak up and judge fairly; defend the rights of the poor and needy" (Proverbs 31:8-9).

"If a man shuts his ears to the cry of the poor, he too will cry out and not be answered" (Proverbs 21:13).

"He who despises his neighbor sins, but blessed is he who is kind to the needy" (Proverbs 14:21).

"Always keep on praying for all the saints" (Ephesians 6:18).

Week 4: Prayer for Haiti

Pray for the government of Haiti to be able to respond to the needs of its people and to find and implement long-term solutions to the hunger and other issues in Haiti.

Pray for those who are hungry in Haiti right now. Pray that God would provide for them and sustain them.

Cry out with the Haitians for the healing of their land. Pray that God would help restore the deforested land of Haiti and that solutions would be found to the agricultural needs of the country. Pray for education in sustainable agricultural practices.

Pray for God to raise up God-following and wise political leaders in Haiti. Pray for the stability of the government so that it can care for the needs of its people.

Pray for the church in Haiti. Pray for God-led leaders to be raised up in the church, and pray for the growth of the church as they share the hope that can be found in Jesus.

Pray for those who need clean water in Haiti. Pray for the provision of clean water and education for mothers and caregivers on how to respond to water-borne illnesses, especially diarrhea.

Week 5: Prayer for Thailand

"Whoever welcomes one of these little children in my name welcomes me" (Mark 9:37).

Pray for the Thai government and an end to corruption.

Pray for the Thai church.

Pray for the drug problems in Thailand.

Pray for the separatist insurgency in the south of Thailand.

Pray for those at risk of being exploited.

Week 5: Prayer for Thailand

Pray for corruption to be weeded out of the Thai government. Pray that the government's first priority would be protecting and helping its people. Pray for wise and God-led leaders to arise who could move Thailand into a new era.

Pray for those who are currently in a situation of exploitation. Pray that God would comfort and strengthen them. Pray that God would send others to rescue them.

Pray for those who are caught in a life of dependence on drugs. Pray again for the government, that wise and God-following leaders would be raised up who could respond to end the cycle of violence and destruction involved in the transport and use of drugs.

Pray for the Holy Spirit to empower the church in Thailand to share the gospel of Christ. Pray for a transformation of the culture through a turning to God. Pray for the strength and unity of the small church in Thailand.

Pray for the women and children who are at risk of being exploited or trafficked. Pray for leaders to be raised up who can speak out on their behalf. Pray that they would be educated on the risks of trafficking. Pray for the change of hearts of communities who have been complicit in trafficking.
Pray also for those who have been rescued out of sexual exploitation. Pray that they would receive the aftercare and counseling they need to be reintegrated into society and that they would experience God's healing.

Pray for the safety and protection of those living in the south of Thailand who are threatened by the separatist insurgency. Pray for peace and a lasting solution to this problem.

Week 6: Prayer for Bolivia

"Speak up for those who cannot speak for themselves, for the rights of all who are destitute. Speak up and judge fairly; defend the rights of the poor and needy" (Proverbs 31:8-9).

"Seek justice, encourage the oppressed. Defend the cause of the fatherless, plead the case of the widow" (Isaiah 1:17).

"If anyone gives even a cup of cold water to one of these little ones because he is my disciple, I tell you the truth, he will certainly not lose his reward" (Matthew 10:42).

"Have nothing to do with the fruitless deeds of darkness, but rather expose them" (Ephesians 5:11).

"I know that the Lord secures justice for the poor and upholds the cause of the needy" (Psalm 140:12).

"Train a child in the way he should go, and when he is old he will not turn from it" (Proverbs 22:6).

Week 6: Prayer for Bolivia

Child Laborers

Pray for the children in Bolivia who are laborers and for those in danger of being trafficked as laborers who do not have an opportunity for education. Pray for laws to protect child laborers. Pray for a transformation of families in Bolivia so parents would advocate for their children.

Violence Against Children

Pray that the Holy Spirit would use the church in Bolivia to transform the culture of violence against children and that children's advocacy groups in Bolivia would be effective in impacting the culture and creating laws to protect the rights of children. Pray that God would comfort, protect, and provide for children who are currently suffering.

Drug Trade

Pray for the protection of the children who would be exploited by the drug trade. Pray that the church would be a safe place for children who might otherwise be attracted to gangs. Pray that the Holy Spirit would transform and heal this country and protect the children.

Child Mortality

Pray for education for mothers to learn how to keep their children healthy. Pray for economic opportunity for the families who struggle to feed their children each day.

Families

Pray for a transformation of families in Bolivia. Pray that the Holy Spirit would use the church to transform the culture so fathers would support their wives and children and so the rights of children would be embraced.

Economic and Political Stability

Pray for stability so this resource-rich country can gain economic and investment opportunities to alleviate the country's poverty. Pray for good infrastructure and governance so this country can end poverty.

Week 7: Prayer for Afghanistan

The Results of War and Instability

The Drug Trade

Oppression of Women and Human Rights Violations

Food Insecurity

Religious Persecution

The Church

Week 7: Prayer for Afghanistan

Pray for the end of the drug trade. Pray for legitimate work for the workers to transfer to and leaders to fight government corruption. Pray for the restoration of other crops. Pray for the trade to switch to legal trade, such as trade in medicinal morphine.

Pray for peace, stability, and unity in Afghanistan. Pray for investment and development in the country so infrastructure can be built. Pray for the development of the educational system so skilled workers can be trained.

Pray for the healing of Afghanistan's land, that subsistence farmers would be able to grow enough to feed their families. Pray for education in good agricultural practices. Pray for the children who are not getting enough food to become healthy, thriving adults. Pray for aid agencies to have access to help those who are suffering the most.

Thank God for the lessening of the burden on women after the ousting of the Taliban. Pray for a transformation of the culture that oppresses women. Pray for education for women and girls. Pray for women teachers and leaders to be raised up and for just laws to be put in place to protect women.

Pray for the millions in Afghanistan who have never had an opportunity to hear the gospel. Pray for the small church that exists, that their number might be added to.

Pray for the strengthening and empowerment of the Christians in Afghanistan. Pray that they would become mature followers of Christ. Pray for their protection against persecution and their boldness in facing it.

Week 8: My Prayer

Dear God,

I thank you that I am your workmanship, created in Christ Jesus to do good works, which you prepared in advance for me to do.

I thank you that you have given me gifts that I might serve others.
I place this gift at your feet:

_____

_____

I ask that you would give me direction in how I can serve you best in this matter:

_____

_____

I commit to take this step in seeking your direction:

_____

_____

I thank you that you always provide for my needs, and I pray that you would continue to provide for me. I want to be used by you as your servant to glorify you. I commit myself to your service.

Signed,

Uganda Cards

Uganda is a tropical country in East Africa, west of Kenya. It's about the size of Oregon.

If you could visit any tropical country in the world, where would you go?

Uganda borders Lake Victoria, the second largest freshwater lake in the world and one of the sources of the Nile.

Tell your favorite lake memory (or if you don't have one, your favorite ocean or river memory).

The borders of Uganda were established when it was colonized by Great Britain. This grouped together a wide range of ethnic groups with different cultures and political systems.

Tell a little about the culture you grew up in—small town? Southern? mining community? What was it like?

About 80% of Ugandans make their living in agriculture, and Uganda's biggest export is coffee.

Do you think you would like being a farmer? Why or why not? (If you are a farmer, tell what it's like!)

Many tourists travel to Uganda each year to go on a gorilla safari.

If you could see any animal in the world in the wild, which would you want to see?

Uganda Cards

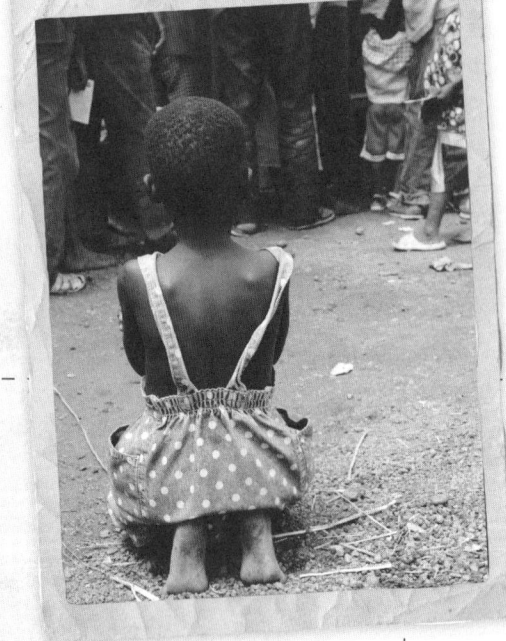

Christian Love in Action

Touch the lives of people in: **Peru, Israel, Thailand, Alaska, Kenya, Guatemala, Ecuador, the Caribbean, and more.** See the world God created, and experience God working in it. Share your Christian love!

Care for children. Serve the elderly. Do community service. Teach orphans. Repair and maintain a school or home. Comfort AIDS babies. **You'll care for the "least of these."** This is important service where your projects are focused on the real needs of people in each location.

Organize a church group. Bring your family and friends, or just yourself. Call 1.800.747.2157 or go to LifetreeAdventures.com to get more information or to customize a service trip.

We'll help you serve and navigate the world.

LifetreeAdventures.com
1.800.747.2157